Rall the Bronze Age Collapse

The Sea Peoples in Legend, History, and Archaeology

R Jay Driskill

Red Pirate Media

RAIDERS OF THE BRONZE AGE COLLAPSE: THE SEA PEOPLES IN LEGEND, HISTORY, AND ARCHAEOLOGY

Copyright © 2025 by R Jay Driskill

Published by Red Pirate Media, New York, NY

All rights reserved. Printed in the United States of America. No part of this book may be used or reproduced in any manner whatsoever without written permission except in the case of brief quotations embodied in critical articles or reviews.

For information contact: Red Pirate Media rjaydriskill.com

All Chapter Photos Courtesy of The Met

Map: "Ancient Near East 1400BC" by Enyavar is licensed under CC BY-SA 4.0.

Library of Congress Control Number: 2025916620

ISBN: 978-1-968989-04-0 Ebook

ISBN: 978-1-968989-05-7 Paperback

ISBN: 978-1-968989-06-4 Hardback

ISBN: 978-1-968989-07-1 Audiobook

First Edition: November 2025

10 9 8 7 6 5 4 3 2 1

Realms of Ancient Near East around 1400 BCE

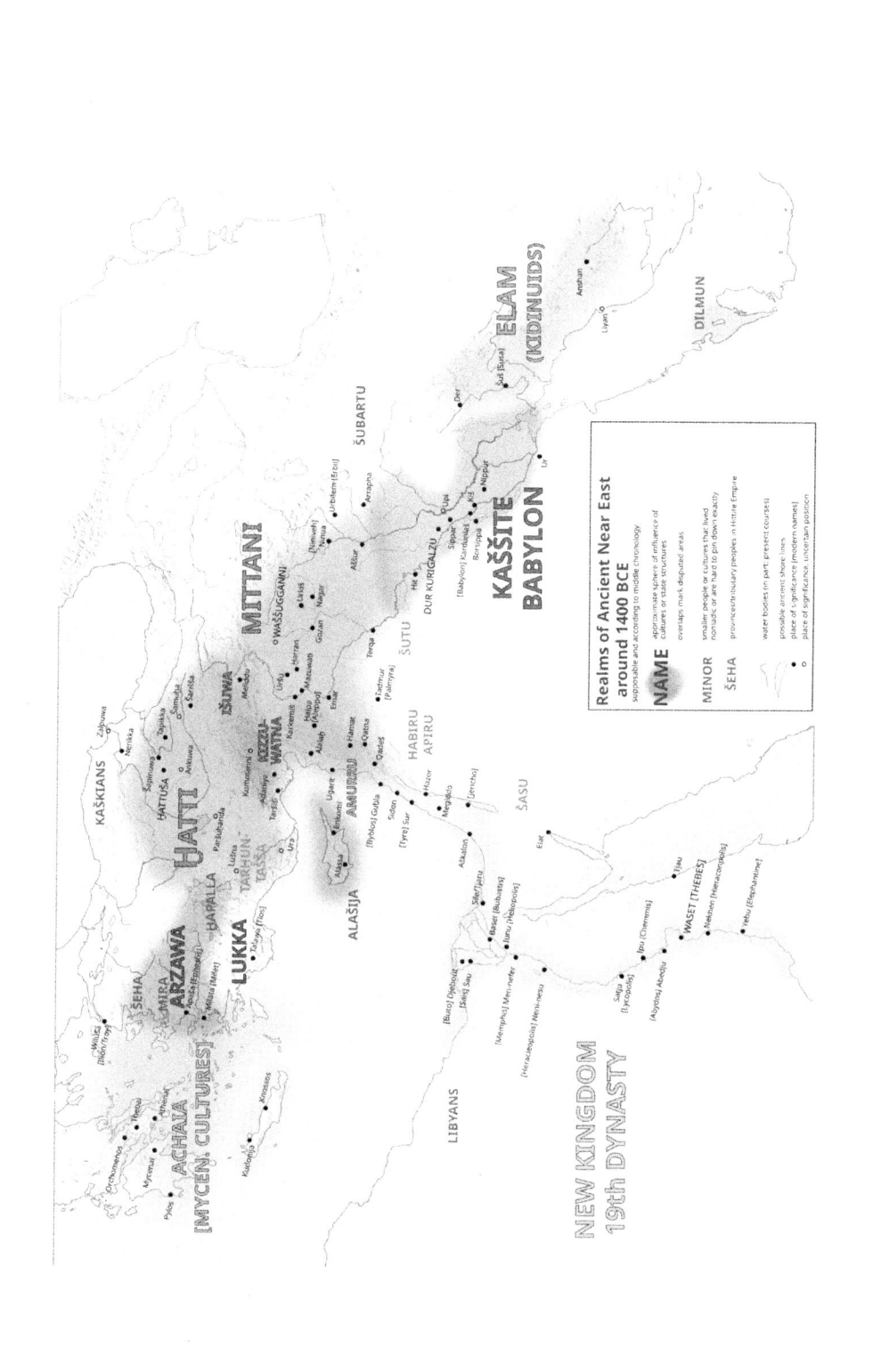

supportable and according to middle chronology

NAME approx. major sphere of influence of cultures or state structures
overlaps mark disputed areas

MINOR smaller people or cultures that lived nomadic, or are hard to pin down exactly

ŠEHA provinces/tributary peoples in Hittite Empire

water bodies (in part, present courses)
possible ancient shore lines
● place of significance (modern names)
○ place of significance, uncertain position

KAŠKIANS
Zalpuwa, Nerikka

HATTI
Šapinuwa, Tapikka, HATTUŠA

ACHAIA
[MYCEN. CULTURES]
Mycenae, Pylos, Thebes, Athens, Orchomenos, Knossos, Kydonia

ŠEHA
MIRA
Apaša [Ephesus]
Millata [Milet]

ARZAWA
HAPALLA
LUKKA
Tarḫun-Tašša
Tatajay [Ticê]

KIZZUWATNA
Kummanni, Adaniya, Tarsaš
Ura
Aḫḫiya [Alassa]

ALAŠIJA

MITTANI
WAŠŠUGANNI
Malitya, Samuḫa, Šeriša
Urkeš, Mer, Nagar, Guzana, Ḫaran
Karkemiš, Ḫalab [Aleppo], Alalaḫ, Emar
Tuttul, Mari

IŠUWA

ŠUBARTU
Urbelum [Erbil]
[Nineveh] Ninua, Arrapḫa
Aššur
Nuzi

AMURRU
Ugarit
[Byblos] Gubla
Sidon
[Tyre] Sur

ḪABIRU
APIRU
Ḥazor
Qadeš
Tadmur [Palmyra]
Qatna
Ḥamat

ŠUTU

DUR KURIGALZU
[Babylon] Karduniaš
Borsippa

KAŠŠITE BABYLON
Sippar, Kiš, Nippur
Ur
Šuš [Susa]

ELAM (KIDINUIDS)
Anšan
Liyan

DILMUN

ŠASU

LIBYANS

NEW KINGDOM 19th DYNASTY
[Buto] Djebaut, [Sais] Sau
[Memphis] Men-nufer, Iunu [Heliopolis]
Saqja [Lycopolis]
[Heracleopolis] Nen-nesu
[Abydos] Abedju
Iunu [Chemenu]
Nekhen [Hieraconpolis]
WASET [THEBES]
Yebu [Elephantine]
Tjau
Eilat
Akakam
[Jericho]
Megiddo

CONTENTS

Also by R Jay Driskill	VII
Epigraph	IX
Preface	1
Introduction: The Glittering Bronze Age World	11
1. Who Were They? Defining the Enigma	35
2. The First Waves: Early Incursions	53
3. The Great Cataclysm: The Reign of Ramesses III	71
4. Beyond Egypt: The Wider Destruction	87
5. The Mechanics of Collapse	103
6. Settling In: The Philistines and Others	119
7. The "Dark Age" and Rebirth	135
8. Enduring Mysteries and Modern Interpretations	155
9. Popular Imagination and Future Directions	167
Appendices:	179
Bibliography	197
Coming Soon...	211
About the author	213

ALSO BY RJAY DRISKILL

SUNSET IN BRONZE SERIES:
KINGS OF STONE: THE HITTITE ENIGMA
RAIDERS OF THE BRONZE AGE COLLAPSE: THE SEA PEOPLES IN LEGEND, HISTORY, AND ARCHAEOLOGY
GHOSTS OF ARZAWA: BEYOND THE TROJAN WAR MYTH
SONG OF A LOST CITY: TROY IN MYTH, FICTION, AND FACT

The Mediterranean is the ocean of history.

Fernand Braudel

PREFACE

The past has always called to me. As a child, I would dig in my mother's garden, not for worms or to plant seeds, but in search of artifacts that might reveal stories of those who came before. Those childhood excavations yielded nothing more than rusty nails and broken china, but they planted a seed that would grow into a lifelong pursuit of understanding human history through what we leave behind.

Growing up in Alabama, history is all around; Native American, Early Settler, Civil War. People who stood on the same ground fascinated me, who stared at the same moon, sun, and stars, but ages before us. Later I became fascinated with World War II, the Great War, Napoleon, Rome, Ancient Greece, and finally the Bronze Age. There's no shortage of mysteries.

Archaeology is detective work across millennia. We piece together fragments—literal and figurative—to reconstruct not just how people lived, but how civilizations rose, interacted, and sometimes collapsed. Few historical mysteries have captivated archaeologists, historians, and the public imagination quite like the enigma of the Sea Peoples. Their shadowy presence at one of history's most pivotal moments has generated debate, speculation, and controversy for over a century (Sandars 1985; Oren 2000; Cline 2014).

This book represents the culmination of years of fieldwork, research, and scholarly exchange. It aims to bring clarity to a historical puzzle that continues to elude definitive explanation, despite—or perhaps because of—the mountain of scholarship devoted to it.

Why the Sea Peoples Matter

The period between 1200 and 1150 BCE witnessed one of the most dramatic systemic collapses in recorded human history (Cline 2014; Ward and Joukowsky 1992). The sophisticated Bronze Age civilizations of the eastern Mediterranean—the Mycenaeans, Hittites, Canaanites, and others—crumbled within a single generation. Cities burned. Trade networks disintegrated. Writing systems disappeared. The Egyptian New Kingdom, while surviving the initial catastrophe, began its long decline (Redford 1992; Shaw 2000).

Amid this chaos appear the mysterious confederations known collectively as the "Sea Peoples"—a term coined by the Egyptians themselves (Breasted 1906; Kitchen 1996). Their arrival coincides with this extraordinary collapse so perfectly that for many decades, scholars assumed a simple causal relationship: the Sea Peoples destroyed Bronze Age civilization (Sandars 1985; Drews 1993).

Reality, as always, proves more complex. Were they invaders or refugees? Destroyers or scapegoats? Pirates or displaced peoples seeking new homes? Were they a coherent group at all, or a convenient Egyptian label for various maritime peoples encountered during a time of crisis (Sherratt 1998; Yasur-Landau 2010; Middleton 2017)?

These questions matter because they speak to fundamental patterns in human history. How do complex societies collapse? What roles do migration, climate change, internal decay, and external pressure play in these processes? The Sea Peoples stand at the intersection of all these questions, making them a crucial case study for understanding not just ancient history, but the fragility and resilience of human societies across time.

The Persistence of the Debate

One might reasonably ask why, after more than a century of archaeological investigation, we still debate the nature and impact of the Sea Peoples. The answer lies partly in the fragmentary nature of our evidence. Unlike the well-documented Roman Empire or even the relatively well-attested civilizations of Egypt and Mesopotamia, the Sea Peoples left us no texts of their own. We know them primarily through the accounts of their enemies and victims—hardly unbiased sources—and through archaeological remains that require careful interpretation (Adams and Cohen 2013; Ben-Dor Evian 2017).

The extraordinary significance compounds this evidentiary challenge attributed to them. The Bronze Age collapse marks the end of the first era of globalization and international diplomacy (Sherratt 2003; Monroe 2009). It represents a systems collapse that transformed the ancient world and set the stage for the emergence of new political forms in the Iron Age. The Sea Peoples have become symbolic actors in this drama, bearing the weight of historical causation perhaps beyond what the evidence can support.

Moreover, the debate persists because it touches on themes that resonate deeply with our present concerns: migration and its affects, climate change and resource scarcity, the vulnerability of interconnected systems, and the resilience of human communities in the face of catastrophic change (Kaniewski et al. 2013; Knapp and Manning 2016). Each generation of scholars approaches the question with new methodologies, technologies, and theoretical frameworks, finding in the Sea Peoples reflections of their own historical moment.

The Structure of This Investigation

This book takes a multidisciplinary approach to the Sea Peoples question, moving beyond traditional archaeological and textual analysis to incorporate insights from climate science, network theory, and comparative anthropology. The investigation unfolds across seven main sections:

First, we examine the primary textual evidence—the Egyptian inscriptions at Medinet Habu and earlier references from the reigns of Merneptah and Ramesses II (Kitchen 1996; Roberts 2009; Ben-Dor Evian 2016). These sources provide our only contemporary written accounts of the Sea Peoples, yet they must be read with an understanding of Egyptian royal ideology and propaganda.

Second, we survey the archaeological evidence for destruction across the eastern Mediterranean at the end of the Late Bronze Age. Site by site, from Troy to Ugarit, from Mycenae to Hattusa, we analyze what the material record tells us about the nature and timing of these catastrophic events (Yon 1992; Zuckerman 2007; Maran 2009).

Third, we consider the evidence for climate change during this period. Recent paleoclimatic data from lake sediments, speleothems, and marine cores suggest a prolonged drought affected the eastern Mediterranean in the late 13th and early 12th centuries BCE (Kaniewski et al. 2010; Kaniewski et al. 2013). We assess how this environmental stress may have contributed to the broader systemic collapse.

Fourth, we examine the material culture associated with the Sea Peoples, particularly the distinctive pottery styles, weapons, and burial practices that appear across the Mediterranean in the collapse's wake (Dothan 1982; Killebrew 2005; Yasur-Landau 2010). These archaeological signatures help us trace population movements and cultural transmissions during this turbulent period.

Fifth, we explore alternative models for understanding the collapse that move beyond simple invasion narratives. Systems collapse theory, network analysis, and comparative studies of other historical collapses offer new frameworks for interpreting the evidence (Middleton 2017; Routledge and McGeough 2009).

Sixth, we follow the aftermath and legacy of the Sea Peoples in the early Iron Age. Some groups, like the Philistines in the Levant, established new polities that would shape the geopolitical landscape for centuries to come (Dothan and Dothan 1992; Stager 1995; Maeir et al. 2013). Others seem to have been absorbed into existing populations, leaving traces in material culture and perhaps in mythological traditions.

Finally, we conclude by synthesizing these diverse lines of evidence into a new understanding of who the Sea Peoples were and what role they played in the Bronze Age collapse—one that acknowledges both their agency as historical actors and the broader structural forces that shaped their movements and actions.

Beyond Simple Narratives

The traditional narrative of the Sea Peoples as a marauding confederation that brought down Bronze Age civilization through military conquest has long been questioned (Sherratt 1998; Yasur-Landau 2010). Yet equally simplistic counter-narratives—that they were merely refugees, or a convenient Egyptian fiction—fail to account for the complexity of the evidence.

My research suggests a more nuanced understanding. The groups collectively labeled "Sea Peoples" by the Egyptians appear to have originated from different regions of the Mediterranean world, including western Anatolia, the Aegean, and possibly parts of southern Europe (Bachhuber 2021; Jung 2018). They were diverse in their origins, motivations, and impacts.

Some groups, facing environmental stress and political instability in their homelands, took to the sea as raiders and pirates, targeting wealthy coastal settlements and shipping (Artzy 1997; Hitchcock and Maeir 2016). Others moved as displaced populations—entire communities seeking new lands to settle after their own territories became unviable because of drought or political collapse.

These movements did not occur in a vacuum. They interacted with and accelerated other processes already underway: the weakening of palatial economies, disruption of trade networks, internal social tensions, and environmental challenges. The Sea Peoples were both products and agents of the collapse—both victims and opportunists in a world undergoing rapid transformation.

This understanding helps explain the archaeological evidence more completely than either invasion or refugee models alone. It accounts both for the destruction layers at numerous sites and for the evidence for more gradual abandonment at others. It explains the appearance of new cultural elements in certain regions alongside clear continuities with earlier traditions (Yasur-Landau 2012; Maeir and Hitchcock 2017).

New Methodologies, New Insights

Recent advances in archaeological science have transformed our ability to track ancient population movements and environmental changes. Strontium isotope analysis of human remains can now reveal whether individuals grew up in the region where they were buried or migrated from elsewhere. Ancient DNA studies, though still limited for this period, offer promising avenues for understanding population movements and admixture.

My own research has focused on transitional sites—places that show evidence of both destruction and continuity, abandonment and reoccupation. These liminal spaces tell us more about the complex processes at work than either completely destroyed sites or those that show uninterrupted occupation.

For example, at Tell Tayinat in southern Turkey, there is a clear transition from Hittite to new cultural forms associated with the Sea Peoples, but with evidence for cooperation and integration rather than simple replacement (Janeway 2006-2007; Janeway 2017). Similar patterns appear at sites across Cyprus and the northern Levant, suggesting that in many places, newcomers and local populations forged new hybrid communities in the aftermath of political collapse (Kopanias 2017; Pedrazzi 2013).

Climate proxy data from Cyprus indicates a sharp decline in rainfall beginning around 1200 BCE, with conditions not improving until nearly a century later (Kaniewski et al. 2013). This aligns with evidence from Syria, Greece, and Anatolia, painting a picture of regional environmental stress that would have impacted agricultural production and potentially triggered population movements.

Network analysis of Late Bronze Age trade connections reveals how the highly specialized, interdependent economies of this period created systemic vulnerabilities (Routledge and McGeough 2009; Monroe 2009). When key nodes in these networks failed—whether through environmental stress, internal conflict, or external attack—the effects cascaded through the system, affecting even regions not directly experiencing crisis.

Why This Matters Beyond Academia

The story of the Sea Peoples and the Bronze Age collapse is not merely an academic puzzle. It offers vital lessons for our own increasingly interconnected and environmentally stressed world.

The Late Bronze Age represented one of humanity's first experiments with globalization—a network of trade, diplomacy, and cultural exchange that spanned the known world (Sherratt 2003; Feldman 2006). Its collapse reminds us that complex systems can be fragile, and that multiple stressors can combine in unexpected ways to trigger cascading failures.

The role of climate change in this historical drama resonates with our contemporary challenges. The Late Bronze Age societies faced climate shifts they could neither fully understand nor control, forcing adaptation, migration, and, in some cases, conflict over dwindling resources (Kaniewski et al. 2013; Manning 2013). Their experiences offer a case study in how human societies respond to environmental change—sometimes with resilience and innovation, sometimes with collapse.

The migration aspects of the Sea Peoples phenomenon speak to ongoing debates about human mobility in times of crisis. Then, as now, population movements could bring both conflict and creative fusion, destruction and renewal. The archaeological record shows communities that failed and vanished alongside others that integrated newcomers and thrived (Yasur-Landau 2012; Emanuel 2013).

Perhaps most importantly, the Bronze Age collapse and subsequent recovery demonstrate human resilience. The destruction was not an end but a transformation. New political forms emerged—smaller, more flexible, and in some ways more innovative than the palace-centered states they replaced. The alphabetic writing systems that would transform human communication developed in this post-collapse environment. Iron technology, more accessible than bronze, spread widely. The foundations for the classical world were laid in the ashes of Bronze Age civilization (Dickinson 2006; Wengrow 2010).

A Personal Reflection

My journey with the Sea Peoples began with the massive relief carvings at Medinet Habu in Egypt. There, carved in stone, were the enemies of Ramesses III—distinctive in their feathered headdresses and unusual weapons (Roberts 2008; Ben-Dor Evian 2016). They seemed so alien, so other, in Egyptian artistic convention. Yet the accompanying texts described a desperate struggle for survival, not just glory-seeking military conquest.

In the decades since, I've studied sites across the Mediterranean that bear witness to this pivotal moment in history. I've studied pottery made during the final days of once-great cities, uncovered buildings destroyed in ancient conflicts, and studied human remains that tell stories of violence, displacement, and resilience.

What began as an archaeological question has expanded into an exploration of how human societies function under stress—how they break, adapt, and rebuild. The Sea Peoples were not simply destroyers or victims; they were people navigating a changing world with the resources and understanding available to them. Some responded with violence, others with flight, still others with innovation and adaptation.

This more human understanding of the Sea Peoples doesn't diminish their historical significance. Rather, it places them within a complex web of causation that includes climate change, political fragility, economic interdependence, and human agency. They remain crucial actors in one of history's great transformations, but actors responding to circumstances partly beyond their control, making choices that made sense in their context.

As we face our own era of rapid change, environmental challenge, and political uncertainty, the story of the Sea Peoples reminds us that human history is neither a tale of inevitable progress nor one of predetermined collapse. It is a continuing conversation between human choices and the larger forces that shape our world—a conversation we can better understand by listening carefully to the voices of the past, even when they speak to us only through fragments of pottery, layers of ash, and the biased accounts of their adversaries.

In the pages that follow, I invite you to join me in piecing together one of history's great puzzles—not just to solve an ancient mystery, but to better understand the patterns that continue to shape our human journey. The Sea Peoples may belong to the distant past, but the questions their story raises remain urgently contemporary: How do societies respond to crisis? What happens when established systems fail? And how do we build something new from the remains of the old?

These questions have no simple answers, either in the Bronze Age or today. But by examining them through the lens of archaeology—through the tangible remains of human lives and choices—we can perhaps find wisdom to guide our own responses to an uncertain future.

R Jay Driskill

June 2025

R JAY DRISKILL

INTRODUCTION: THE GLITTERING BRONZE AGE WORLD

The Interconnected Mediterranean

Long before the mysterious Sea Peoples appeared on the horizon, the eastern Mediterranean flourished in what scholars now call the Late Bronze Age. From approximately 1550 to 1200 BCE, this region hosted a remarkable network of civilizations—powerful, sophisticated, and intricately connected (Cline 2014; Broodbank 2013). To understand the magnitude of what would eventually collapse, we must first appreciate what had been built.

The Aegean world sparkled with Mycenaean palaces, stone-built centers of political power, economic production, and cultural achievement (Kelder 2010; Dickinson 2006). At Mycenae itself, massive "Cyclopean" walls—named for their enormous stones that later Greeks believed only the mythical one-eyed giants could have moved—surrounded a citadel where a warrior elite controlled surrounding territories. These imposing fortifications, some blocks weighing over twenty tons, protected elaborate megaron-style palaces with columned porticoes and vibrant frescoed walls. Similar centers at Tiryns, Pylos, and elsewhere formed a loose confederation of Greek-speaking kingdoms (Davis 2008). Their distinctive pottery, characterized by elegant marine and geometric motifs rendered in lustrous dark paint, has been found throughout the Mediterranean, testifying to their extensive trade networks (Mountjoy 1998), while their administrative records—preserved on clay tablets in the Linear B script—reveal a highly organized society with specialized craftspeople, religious officials, and military forces.

To the east, the Hittite Empire dominated Anatolia from its capital at Hattusa, a sprawling city of imposing temples and defensive works nestled among the rugged hills of central Turkey (Bryce 2005). The city's massive walls, punctuated by elaborately decorated gates featuring lions and sphinxes, enclosed a complex of temples, palaces, and administrative buildings that served as the nerve center of an empire. The Hittite kings styled themselves as "Great Kings," equals to the pharaohs of Egypt, and maintained a complex diplomatic and military apparatus that managed relations with vassal states and rival powers (Beckman 1999). Their archives, preserved on thousands of clay tablets written in cuneiform, document a sophisticated legal system, international treaties, and religious practices that incorporated elements from the many cultures under their rule (Hoffner 2009). The Hittite legal code, with its relatively lenient punishments and concern for proportional justice, reflects a pragmatic approach to governance that helped maintain stability across their diverse territories.

Egypt, under the New Kingdom pharaohs of the 18th and 19th Dynasties, experienced a period of unprecedented wealth and international influence (Shaw 2000; Redford 1992). From their capitals at Thebes and Pi-Ramesses, they controlled territories stretching from Nubia in the south to parts of the Levant in the northeast. The magnificent temples at Karnak and Luxor, with their soaring columns and vast hypostyle halls, dominated the landscape along the life-giving Nile. The tombs in the Valley of the Kings, with their elaborate wall paintings depicting the afterlife journey, and the statuary and luxury goods produced for the elite represent the pinnacle of Egyptian artistic achievement. Their diplomatic correspondence, preserved in the Amarna Letters, reveals Egypt's central position in the international system of the day, where pharaohs exchanged pleasantries, gifts, and sometimes thinly veiled threats with fellow rulers across the known world (Moran 1992).

Between these great powers lay smaller but culturally significant kingdoms. The city-states of the Levant, including Ugarit, Byblos, and Tyre, served as crucial trading hubs where Egyptian, Mesopotamian, Aegean, and Anatolian influences mingled in a vibrant cultural exchange (Singer 1999; Yon 1992). Perched on the eastern Mediterranean coast, these cities featured bustling harbors where ships from across the sea would dock, unloading exotic cargo and foreign visitors. At Ugarit, archaeologists have uncovered archives written in multiple languages and scripts, evidence of a cosmopolitan society where merchants from across the known world conducted business in specialized commercial districts (Pardee 2003; Schaeffer 1968). The biblical Canaanites, often portrayed as enemies of the Israelites, were in fact sophisticated urbanites with connections spanning the Mediterranean, living in cities with advanced water management systems, multi-story buildings, and specialized craft workshops producing fine textiles, carved ivory, and metalwork that combined techniques and motifs from multiple cultural traditions.

Cyprus, rich in copper—the crucial component of bronze—played a special role in this interconnected world (Knapp 2013; Karageorghis 1992). Its strategic position and valuable resources made it a nexus of trade and cultural exchange. The distinctive oxhide-shaped copper ingots produced on the island have been found in shipwrecks and settlements throughout the region, standardized for international trade. Cypriot pottery, with its characteristic red polished surfaces or black-on-red decoration, appears in archaeological contexts throughout the region, while imported goods from mainland Greece, Egypt, and the Levant testify to the island's centrality to Bronze Age commerce. The island's settlements featured substantial buildings with ashlar masonry, elaborate tombs filled with imported luxury goods, and sanctuaries where local and foreign religious practices blended into syncretic forms of worship.

Even distant Sardinia took part in this network, exporting copper and other goods and importing techniques and styles from the eastern Mediterranean (Vagnetti 2000). The distinctive Nuragic culture of Bronze Age Sardinia, with its unique stone towers rising like sentinels across the landscape, developed in dialogue with these wider Mediterranean influences. Archaeological evidence shows Sardinian raw materials reaching Egypt and the Levant, while Mycenaean and Cypriot pottery found on the island demonstrates the reach of eastern Mediterranean trading networks into the central Mediterranean basin.

This was a world bound together by seaborne trade, diplomatic ties, and cultural exchange—a proto-globalized network that would not be matched in complexity until the Classical period centuries later (Sherratt 2003; Feldman 2006). Royal courts exchanged letters written on clay tablets or papyrus, carried by messengers who traveled for weeks or months to deliver them. They sent gifts of gold, lapis lazuli, carved ivory, and fine textiles to cement alliances, and arranged marriages between royal families to create bonds of kinship across political boundaries. Merchants moved goods across political boundaries in ships capable of carrying tons of cargo, navigating by stars and seasonal winds, stopping at established ports where they knew they would find markets and supplies (Bachhuber 2021). Artists borrowed motifs and techniques from foreign traditions, adapting sphinxes, griffins, palm trees, and lotus flowers to local tastes. Craftspeople shared technological innovations in metallurgy, glassmaking, textile production, and architecture, creating a material culture that combined distinctive local elements with international styles.

The material evidence for this interconnection appears throughout the archaeological record. Mycenaean pottery, with its distinctive shapes and decoration, has been found in Egyptian tombs, Levantine households, and Cypriot sanctuaries—sometimes containing perfumed oils or wine, sometimes adopted for local use in ways its makers never intended. Cypriot copper circulated widely, fashioned into tools and weapons in workshops across the region, from the sword-smiths of Mycenae to the bronze casters of Egypt. Egyptian scarabs and amulets traveled to the Aegean, where they were sometimes incorporated into local jewelry or burial practices with little understanding of their original religious significance. Ugaritic texts mention goods from across the known world—timber from Lebanon, horses from Anatolia, textiles from Mesopotamia, ivory from Africa—passing through their port en route to distant destinations. A shipwreck discovered off the coast of Turkey at Uluburun contained cargo from at least seven different cultures—copper and tin ingots, Egyptian jewelry, Mycenaean pottery, Baltic amber, and African ivory—a snapshot of Bronze Age cosmopolitanism frozen in time when the vessel sank around 1300 BCE (Bass et al. 1989; Pulak 1998; Bachhuber 2006).

The written evidence is equally compelling. The Amarna Letters—diplomatic correspondence between Egypt and various Near Eastern powers—reveal a world where rulers addressed each other as "brother" and negotiated exchanges of gold, silver, and royal women (Moran 1992; Goren et al. 2004). Written in Akkadian, the diplomatic lingua franca of the day, these clay tablets preserve the sometimes flowery, sometimes testy exchanges between kings who saw themselves as peers in an exclusive international club. Hittite treaties detail complex diplomatic arrangements with vassal states, specifying tribute payments, military obligations, extradition procedures, and even provisions for political refugees (Beckman 1999). Mycenaean administrative texts record the distribution of resources and the organization of labor, listing precise amounts of grain, olive oil, and wool allocated to palace dependents, from high-ranking officials to humble workers. Together, these sources depict societies of remarkable administrative sophistication, capable of managing complex economic systems and international relationships through bureaucracies staffed by professional scribes and administrators.

This was not merely a world of elite exchange. Ordinary people participated in these networks as well. Merchants of middling status traveled between cultural zones, sometimes settling in foreign ports where they formed distinct communities with their own customs and commercial practices. Craftspeople adapted foreign techniques to local tastes, creating hybrid styles that appealed to consumers looking for both novelty and familiarity. Common household goods—cooking pots, oil lamps, textile tools—show patterns of regional interaction alongside distinctive local traditions, as practical innovations spread through observation and imitation. Religious ideas and practices moved along the same routes as material goods, creating syncretic belief systems that incorporated elements from multiple traditions. Storm gods, fertility goddesses, and divine craftsmen appeared in multiple pantheons under different names but with recognizable attributes and stories.

The Late Bronze Age world was not, of course, a peaceful utopia. Wars were frequent, particularly along the frontiers where great powers met. The Battle of Kadesh in 1274 BCE between the Egyptians under Ramesses II and the Hittites under Muwatalli II represents one of history's first well-documented military engagements—a massive clash involving thousands of chariots and tens of thousands of infantry that ended in stalemate and eventually a formal peace treaty (Kitchen 1996; Edel 1994). Mycenaean texts mention military preparations and coastal watchtowers, suggesting ongoing concerns about security in a world where piracy and raiding were common occurrences. Fortifications around cities throughout the region testify to the reality of armed conflict, with some settlements showing evidence of multiple destructions and rebuildings over relatively short periods.

Yet these conflicts occurred within a shared diplomatic framework. Wars ended with treaties rather than annihilation, the terms negotiated by professional diplomats familiar with precedent and protocol. Defeated enemies became vassals rather than slaves, maintaining their distinct identity while acknowledging the suzerainty of their conqueror. The great powers recognized each other's legitimacy and operated according to common understandings of how international relations should function, with established procedures for everything from royal marriages to border disputes. When Ramesses II and Hattusili III of the Hittites signed their famous peace treaty around 1258 BCE, copies were created in both Egyptian hieroglyphics and Akkadian cuneiform—a bilingual document for a multilingual world, displayed prominently in temples to be witnessed by the gods who guaranteed its provisions (Beckman 1999).

This interconnected system reached its peak in the 14th and 13th centuries BCE. The material culture of this period shows unprecedented standardization across cultural boundaries, with certain pottery types, architectural features, and artistic motifs appearing throughout the region. Administrative systems grew increasingly complex, with specialized bureaucracies managing everything from agricultural production to international trade. International trade reached new heights of volume and sophistication, with dedicated port facilities, standardized weights and measures, and complex financial arrangements including credit and consignment sales (Monroe 2009; Routledge and McGeough 2009). From the perspective of elites in the great palaces and temples, the world must have seemed orderly, prosperous, and permanent—a stable system that had weathered occasional disruptions and would continue indefinitely.

Yet beneath this glittering surface, stresses built that would eventually bring the entire system crashing down. The very complexity and interconnection that had created such remarkable prosperity also created vulnerabilities that would prove catastrophic when multiple crises converged.

Cracks in the Foundation

The first signs of trouble appeared not as dramatic invasions or sudden catastrophes, but as subtle shifts in climate, politics, and social relations—changes that might have seemed manageable in isolation but would prove devastating in combination (Knapp and Manning 2016).

Climate researchers examining ice cores from Greenland, sediment cores from lakes and seas, and pollen samples from archaeological sites have identified a significant shift toward drier conditions throughout the eastern Mediterranean beginning around 1300 BCE (Kaniewski et al. 2010; Kaniewski et al. 2013). The isotope ratios preserved in these ancient environmental records tell a story of declining rainfall and increasing temperatures across the region. Tree-ring studies from areas as distant as Ireland and China confirm a widespread climate anomaly during this period, suggesting a major disruption in global atmospheric patterns. The evidence suggests a prolonged drought that affected agricultural production across multiple regions simultaneously, with particularly severe impacts in marginal areas where farming had always been precarious.

For societies dependent on grain surpluses to feed specialized urban populations, religious establishments, and military forces, this climate shift represented an existential threat. The Hittite archives contain increasingly desperate letters from one king to another requesting grain shipments: "It is a matter of life or death!" declares one such message, the cuneiform signs pressed urgently into the clay tablet (Hoffner 2009; Singer 2000). Egyptian records from the reign of Merneptah (1213-1203 BCE) mention the shipment of grain to the Hittites "to keep alive the land of Hatti"—an extraordinary admission of vulnerability from one of the ancient world's most powerful states, recorded in hieroglyphics on temple walls that normally boasted only of victories and divine favor (Kitchen 1996).

The effects of drought cascaded through these complex societies. Reduced agricultural output meant less surplus to support craft specialists, scribes, priests, and soldiers—the very personnel who maintained the administrative, religious, and military systems that defined Bronze Age states. Farmers struggling to feed their families had little left to render as taxes or tribute. Tax revenues declined as harvests failed and peasants fled unproductive land. Labor for monumental building projects became harder to mobilize when basic subsistence demanded all available hands. Religious institutions, which legitimized royal authority through elaborate rituals and imposing temples, faced resource shortages that undermined their ritual activities and diminished their spiritual authority.

Archaeological evidence from multiple sites reveals adaptations to these challenging conditions. At Mycenaean palaces, storage capacity increased dramatically, with new facilities constructed to hold grain, olive oil, wine, and other commodities—suggesting efforts to centralize and control diminishing resources (Middleton 2010). Hittite settlements show signs of agricultural intensification—terracing on hillsides to prevent soil erosion, irrigation works to maximize water efficiency, and expansion into marginal lands previously considered unsuitable for cultivation—attempts to maintain production levels despite environmental constraints. In the Levant, archaeologists have documented shifts in crop selection toward more drought-resistant varieties like barley (which requires less water than wheat) and innovations in water management, including cisterns and channeling systems to capture seasonal rainfall.

These adaptations might have succeeded had environmental stress been the only challenge. But the Late Bronze Age world faced multiple, interconnected pressures that compounded one another in a dangerous feedback loop.

Population growth during the prosperous earlier Bronze Age had created demographic pressure throughout the region. Archaeological surveys reveal expansion of settlement into previously unoccupied areas, intensification of land use with fields under cultivation extending farther from settlements, and growing urban populations housed in increasingly dense neighborhoods. This demographic expansion had already strained resources before climate change exacerbated the situation. In some regions, particularly the Aegean and parts of Anatolia, population may have exceeded the carrying capacity of the land even under optimal conditions, requiring a constant flow of imported food to maintain stability.

The complex economic interdependence that had been a source of strength became a vulnerability when multiple nodes in the network experienced simultaneous disruption. When drought affected grain production in the Aegean, the Mycenaean palaces could no longer export olive oil and wine in exchange for food imports, creating shortages of both food and the valuable trade goods that secured their political alliances. When Cypriot copper mines reduced output due to labor shortages or political disruption, bronze production throughout the region suffered, affecting everything from agricultural tools to military equipment. When Ugaritic merchants could not safely travel their usual routes due to piracy or local conflicts, luxury goods stopped flowing to royal courts that depended on such items to reward loyal supporters and maintain their prestige in a competitive international environment.

These economic stresses exposed and exacerbated social tensions within Bronze Age societies. The palace-centered economies of the period were fundamentally extractive—they concentrated resources in the hands of elites while demanding labor and agricultural surplus from the general population. Elaborate administrative systems tracked these obligations down to minute details; Linear B tablets from Mycenaean palaces record precise quantities of grain, oil, and wool owed by specific communities, while Hittite texts specify the labor services required from different categories of royal dependents. This arrangement functioned during times of plenty but generated resentment when resources became scarce and palace demands remained rigid. Archaeological evidence from several Mycenaean centers suggests internal conflict prior to their final destruction—walls dividing parts of cities that previously had open circulation, valuable items hidden in unusual locations suggesting fear of theft or confiscation, hasty burials within settlement areas contrary to normal practices (Maran 2009).

The Linear B tablets from Pylos, preserved when fire baked the clay, document increasing anxiety among the ruling class in the final years before the palace's destruction. They record unusual religious ceremonies, perhaps attempts to appease angry deities believed to be causing the mounting crises. They detail the redistribution of bronze from religious objects to weaponry, indicating both material shortages and security concerns. They list coastal watchers positioned at specific points along the shoreline to provide early warning of seaborne threats, with careful notation of which units are present and which positions remain unmanned. Most tellingly, they show the palace attempting to tighten its control over resources and population at precisely the moment when its ability to provide security and prosperity was most in question—a common but often counterproductive response to weakening authority.

Similar patterns appear in Hittite records from the final decades before the collapse of their capital at Hattusa (Otten 1963; Güterbock 1992). Royal correspondence mentions food shortages severe enough to prompt population movements away from unproductive areas, military threats from multiple directions requiring simultaneous defensive preparations, and diplomatic isolation as former allies became preoccupied with their own crises. Administrative texts show attempts to reorganize territories and extract resources more efficiently, with new officials appointed to oversee troubled provinces and revised tax assessments attempting to match obligations to diminished capabilities. Religious documents reveal new ritual practices, possibly responses to perceived divine disfavor, including elaborate ceremonies involving the royal family and unprecedented offerings to deities associated with weather and fertility. The picture that emerges is of a government struggling to maintain control as its resource base shrinks and its legitimacy erodes—employing every administrative, military, and religious tool at its disposal, yet unable to reverse the deteriorating situation.

In Egypt, the late 19th and early 20th Dynasties faced their own internal challenges (Weinstein 1992). The massive building programs of Ramesses II—including the temples at Abu Simbel, Karnak, and his new capital at Pi-Ramesses—had strained the economy, requiring enormous resources and labor mobilization that left little reserve capacity for crises. His extraordinarily long reign (1279-1213 BCE) created succession problems, with multiple generations of potential heirs competing for position and several of his sons predeceasing him. The centralized bureaucracy that had efficiently managed resources during the height of Egyptian power grew increasingly corrupt and factionalized, with officials carving out personal fiefdoms and diverting resources from royal projects. Archaeological evidence from this period shows a decline in quality in royal construction projects and luxury goods, suggesting resource constraints or administrative failures. Tomb paintings and inscriptions maintain the fiction of eternal prosperity and divine order, but the material reality visible in the archaeological record tells a different story of diminishing capabilities and growing stress.

Even as these internal stresses mounted, external security threats increased. The balance of power that had maintained relative stability among the great kingdoms began to shift. The Assyrian Empire, previously a secondary player in the international system, grew increasingly assertive under Tukulti-Ninurta I (1243-1207 BCE), exploiting Hittite weakness to expand westward and threatening established spheres of influence. The Hittites faced pressure from the Kaska people to their north, semi-nomadic groups who had long raided Hittite territory but now posed a more serious threat to a weakened empire, and various vassal states that sensed weakness in their overlord and tested the limits of their subordination. Egypt confronted challenges from Libya to the west, where tribal groups pressed against the Nile Delta with increasing frequency and force, and Nubia to the south, where the formerly subject territories showed signs of growing independence.

Maritime trade, the lifeblood of the interconnected Bronze Age world, became increasingly risky as piracy increased in the power vacuums created by weakening state control. Ugaritic letters mention ships lost to raiders operating from small islands or remote coastal areas beyond the reach of palace authorities. Egyptian texts describe naval battles against seaborne enemies years before the famous confrontation with the Sea Peoples, suggesting a gradual escalation of maritime insecurity rather than a sudden crisis. Cypriot and Mycenaean settlements show increasing fortification of coastal areas, with watchtowers, defensive walls, and sometimes the abandonment of exposed harbors in favor of more defensible locations. The archaeological record reveals a significant decline in imported goods at many sites in the late 13th century BCE, suggesting disruption of traditional trade routes as merchants avoided increasingly dangerous sea lanes or lacked the capital to risk valuable cargoes in uncertain conditions.

Perhaps most significantly, population movements—both organized migrations and refugee flows—began to destabilize established political arrangements. Hittite texts mention people called the Lukka (possibly from southwestern Anatolia) engaging in seaborne raids against coastal settlements, sometimes in coordination with local rebellions against Hittite authority (Beckman et al. 2011). Egyptian records describe defeating the Sherden (perhaps from Sardinia) at sea, then incorporating them into their military forces as mercenaries—a pattern of confrontation followed by integration that suggests complex relationships rather than simple invasion (Ben-Dor Evian 2017). Ugaritic letters report people arriving from elsewhere in the Levant, fleeing drought or conflict, creating pressure on local resources and social tensions in receiving communities. These movements—initially manageable—would eventually accelerate into the mass migrations associated with the Sea Peoples, as increasingly desperate groups moved in search of security and subsistence.

The cumulative effect of these various stresses—environmental, economic, social, political, and military—was to push the Bronze Age system toward a tipping point where normal adaptive mechanisms would prove insufficient. The centralized, hierarchical, and interdependent nature of these societies, once a source of remarkable achievement, now made them vulnerable to cascading failures. When resources became scarce, central authorities lost the ability to reward supporters and coerce compliance, weakening the bonds that held complex political structures together. When trade networks faltered, specialized production collapsed, eliminating not just luxury goods but essential tools and materials. When legitimacy eroded, social cohesion disintegrated, making coordinated responses to crises impossible.

By approximately 1225 BCE, this process had advanced to a critical stage, though catastrophic collapse was not yet inevitable. The great powers had faced challenges before and developed resilient institutions capable of adaptation. Had the stresses been fewer, more gradual, or less interconnected, the Bronze Age system might have evolved rather than collapsed. Indeed, some regions—notably Egypt and Assyria—would survive the coming storm, albeit in diminished form, preserving elements of Bronze Age civilization into the new era.

But for much of the eastern Mediterranean, the breaking point was approaching. The complex, interconnected civilization that had developed over centuries would soon face a series of shocks that would overwhelm its adaptive capacity. The glittering Bronze Age world stood on the brink of a transformation more profound and far-reaching than any of its inhabitants could have imagined—a transformation that would erase entire political systems, writing traditions, and cultural complexes, creating a historical discontinuity that scholars still struggle to fully comprehend.

The First Dominoes Fall

The archaeological record allows us to trace the sequence of collapse with remarkable precision. Unlike many historical processes that unfold gradually over generations, the Bronze Age collapse occurred within a single human lifetime—roughly from 1225 to 1175 BCE (Cline 2014; Middleton 2017). This compressed timeframe makes it possible to identify not just the general causes but the specific sequence of events that transformed the Mediterranean world.

The first major center to fall was the Mycenaean palace at Thebes in Greece, destroyed by fire around 1225 BCE. Archaeological excavations have revealed a layer of intense burning throughout the administrative complex, with collapsed roof beams, melted storage jars, and baked clay tablets attesting to the ferocity of the blaze. Archaeological evidence suggests intentional destruction rather than natural disaster—the deliberate burning of administrative buildings and storage facilities, while some residential areas were less severely affected. Whether this resulted from external attack, internal conflict, or some combination remains unclear, but the pattern—targeted destruction of elite and administrative structures—would be repeated at sites across the region in the coming decades. The systematic nature of the destruction suggests organized action rather than random violence, possibly indicating social revolution, factional conflict among elites, or a calculated attack aimed at eliminating political authority rather than simply plundering wealth.

Within approximately 15 years, several other Mycenaean centers had suffered similar fates. The palace at Iolkos burned around 1220 BCE, its ruins containing evidence of valuable objects abandoned in the final evacuation, suggesting a hasty departure by its occupants. Gla, with its massive fortifications and complex hydraulic works that had regulated the waters of Lake Kopais for generations, was abandoned with little sign of violent destruction—its inhabitants apparently recognizing the inevitable and departing before catastrophe struck. Mycenae itself shows evidence of earthquake damage followed by hasty repairs and then destruction by fire (Nur and Cline 2000). The archaeological layers tell a story of natural disaster compounded by human violence—walls toppled by seismic activity, makeshift barriers erected in their place, and finally the conflagration that ended the palace's existence as a political center. At Tiryns, the archaeological record reveals multiple destruction events and rebuilding efforts, suggesting a prolonged period of instability rather than a single catastrophic attack. The massive Cyclopean walls were repeatedly breached and repaired, with each rebuilding phase showing diminished resources and technical skill, a physical manifestation of declining capabilities in the face of persistent threat.

The Pylos palace complex offers especially detailed evidence of its final days, thanks to the preservation of its administrative archives in the fire that destroyed the site around 1200 BCE. The Linear B tablets reveal a government mobilizing resources for coastal defense, with records of bronze allocated for weapons production, rations for troops stationed at strategic points along the coast, and inventories of military equipment including chariots, armor, and spears. Other tablets document the redistribution of metal from ceremonial objects to weapons production, listing religious items being melted down to create practical tools for defense—a desperate measure that would have been unthinkable in more stable times. Still others record religious rituals, perhaps intended to avert disaster, with offerings to deities and ceremonial banquets that may represent attempts to maintain social cohesion in the face of mounting threats. These measures proved insufficient; the palace burned with such intensity that the clay tablets were accidentally fired into permanence, preserving the administrative records of a society on the brink of extinction. The destruction was complete and final—the palace's administrative system collapsed permanently, its writing tradition disappeared, and its elaborate frescoes and architecture were reduced to rubble and ash.

As the Mycenaean palace system disintegrated, population patterns in Greece changed dramatically (Dickinson 2006). Archaeological surveys document abandonment of many coastal settlements, their inhabitants fleeing maritime raiders or simply the collapse of the economic system that had sustained them, and growth of defensible inland sites, often in mountainous areas with limited agricultural potential but natural protection against attack. Small villages appeared in remote valleys and on easily defended hilltops, with simple architecture and material culture suggesting communities focused on basic subsistence rather than the specialized production and exchange that had characterized the palace period. Overall population declined significantly—by some estimates, up to 75% in certain regions—through some combination of outmigration, conflict, and declining birth rates in conditions of scarcity and insecurity. The elaborate craft production associated with the palaces disappeared almost entirely, with fine pottery, intricate metalwork, and luxury goods replaced by simpler, locally produced items. Monumental building ceased entirely, with no new fortifications, palaces, or tombs constructed for generations. The Linear B writing system, used exclusively for palace administration, vanished completely—a casualty of the political system it had served, creating a period of functional illiteracy that would last for centuries until the adoption of the Phoenician alphabet in the 8th century BCE.

This was not, however, a reversion to primitive conditions. The people who survived the collapse adapted to their new circumstances with remarkable ingenuity. They developed new settlement patterns based on smaller, more self-sufficient communities rather than centralized palace systems. They modified agricultural practices to emphasize resilience over surplus production, with more diverse crops and greater reliance on pastoralism in marginal areas. They maintained essential technologies like pottery production, metalworking, and textile manufacture, even as they abandoned the specialized luxury production of the palace era. What disappeared was not technological capability but the specific social and political organization that had characterized the Mycenaean world—the hierarchical, bureaucratic structure that had concentrated resources and power in the hands of palace elites.

As the Aegean descended into chaos, the effects rippled outward through the interconnected Mediterranean system. Cyprus, closely connected to Mycenaean trade networks, experienced disruption but initial adaptation (Karageorghis 1992; Knapp 2013). Archaeological evidence shows the abandonment of some settlements along the vulnerable coastlines, fortification of others with new defensive walls and watchtowers, and the appearance of Aegean-style pottery made locally—perhaps by refugees from the Mycenaean world who brought their technical skills but had to use local materials. Cypriot copper production declined but continued, redirected toward new markets as old ones disappeared. The island's strategic location and valuable resources ensured its continued importance, but the cosmopolitan character of its Bronze Age settlements gave way to more defensive, inward-looking communities.

In Anatolia, the Hittite Empire faced mounting pressures from multiple directions. Assyrian texts report a significant Hittite defeat around 1210 BCE, with the Assyrian king Tukulti-Ninurta I claiming to have crossed the Euphrates and defeated a Hittite army—a serious incursion into territory the Hittites had long controlled. Internal Hittite documents reveal grain shortages severe enough to prompt appeals to Egypt for food aid, population movements away from areas affected by drought or conflict, and increasing difficulty maintaining control over vassal states that sensed weakness in their overlord and tested the boundaries of their subordination. The empire's western provinces, particularly along the Aegean coast, show archaeological evidence of destruction and abandonment similar to that in Greece—burned palaces, abandoned settlements, and declining population—suggesting that the same forces affecting the Mycenaean world were also impacting Hittite territories.

The final blow came around 1180-1175 BCE when the Hittite capital at Hattusa was systematically destroyed (Güterbock 1992; Singer 2000). Archaeological evidence indicates that the city was largely abandoned before its destruction—administrative buildings emptied of their contents, valuable items removed or deliberately buried, religious objects ritually deposited in temples. The massive archives that had documented centuries of Hittite history were left behind but show signs of careful selection, with particularly valuable or sacred texts apparently removed before the final abandonment. The destruction itself appears methodical rather than frenzied—temples and palaces burned, defensive walls toppled, monumental sculptures defaced, but without evidence of mass casualties or the chaotic distribution of valuable objects that would suggest hasty looting. This suggests either an organized withdrawal by the Hittite leadership or a deliberate, symbolic destruction of the imperial center by its conquerors—a calculated erasure of the symbols of Hittite power rather than a spontaneous act of violence.

With the fall of Hattusa, the Hittite Empire ceased to exist as a political entity. Its territories fragmented into smaller states, some maintaining elements of Hittite culture and political traditions in what archaeologists call the Neo-Hittite kingdoms, others developing new identities or falling under the influence of different cultural spheres (Weeden 2013; Hawkins 2000). The Hittite language and cuneiform writing system disappeared from Anatolia, though related languages and derived writing systems would persist in some Neo-Hittite states of northern Syria. The elaborate diplomatic apparatus that had helped maintain international stability for generations vanished, along with the military force that had balanced against Egyptian power and regulated relations among smaller states.

The collapse of the Hittite Empire removed a major stabilizing force from the international system and created a power vacuum in Anatolia and northern Syria. Population groups displaced by the empire's fall moved southward and eastward, putting pressure on the already stressed kingdoms of the Levant. Some of these movements may have been organized migrations of entire communities seeking new lands, while others likely represented desperate refugees fleeing violence or starvation. Trade routes that had run through Hittite territory were disrupted, further damaging the interconnected economic system of the eastern Mediterranean. Luxury goods, raw materials, and even basic commodities that had flowed along these routes now became scarce, creating shortages that compounded existing economic problems.

The kingdom of Ugarit, a wealthy trading center on the Syrian coast, provides some of our most vivid evidence of the final days of Bronze Age civilization (Yon 1992; Singer 1999). Clay tablets preserved in the destruction of the city include desperate letters sent to allies requesting military assistance: "The enemy ships are already here, they have set fire to my towns and have done very great damage in the country." The urgency is palpable in these messages, with scribes abandoning the formal diplomatic language typical of earlier correspondence in favor of direct appeals for immediate help. Other tablets report grain shortages that had reached critical levels, population movements into and through Ugarit's territory creating social tension and resource competition, and the departure of the king and his ships—perhaps a failed evacuation attempt that left the remaining population to face the approaching catastrophe without leadership.

Archaeological evidence confirms this picture of crisis. The city was systematically destroyed around 1185 BCE, with evidence of intense burning throughout both elite and common areas. Unlike some other sites, Ugarit shows evidence of violence against the population, with human remains found in collapsed buildings and streets—some showing signs of trauma, others appearing to have been trapped by falling structures or overcome by smoke. The destruction was complete and final; Ugarit would never be reoccupied, its location forgotten until rediscovered by archaeologists in 1928. The thick layer of ash and debris that covered the final Bronze Age occupation level would remain undisturbed for over three thousand years, preserving a snapshot of a sophisticated urban center at the moment of its annihilation.

With Ugarit's fall, one of the most important commercial hubs of the Late Bronze Age disappeared. The sophisticated diplomatic, commercial, and cultural networks that had run through the city were severed. The multiple writing systems used there—including Akkadian cuneiform for international correspondence, Ugaritic alphabetic cuneiform for local administration and literature, and occasionally Egyptian hieratic and Cypro-Minoan scripts—fell out of use (Pardee 2003). The cosmopolitan culture that had characterized the city, with its multiple languages, diverse religious practices, and international outlook, vanished. The extensive archives that had recorded everything from international treaties to mythological epics were buried under collapsed buildings, their contents unknown until modern archaeological excavation revealed the literary and historical treasures preserved by catastrophe.

Similar destruction befell other Levantine centers in quick succession. Tell Tweini, Gibala, Tarshish, and Hamath all show evidence of violent destruction between approximately 1190 and 1175 BCE, with archaeological layers revealing intense burning, structural collapse, and sometimes human remains indicating violent death or entrapment (Bell 2006; Fischer 2007). Some, like Ugarit, would never recover, their ruins remaining abandoned for generations or even permanently. Others would eventually be reoccupied, but often after significant gaps and with markedly different material culture, suggesting discontinuity of population or at least of social organization. The archaeological record shows simpler construction techniques, less specialized craft production, and fewer imported goods in these later settlements—all indicators of reduced resources and more limited participation in long-distance trade networks.

Not all regions experienced such complete devastation. The kingdom of Carchemish, a former Hittite vassal state situated on the Euphrates River, survived to become one of the most important Neo-Hittite states, preserving elements of Hittite political structures, artistic traditions, and religious practices into the Iron Age (Weeden 2013; Hawkins 2000). The Phoenician cities of Byblos, Sidon, and Tyre suffered disruption but maintained their urban character and maritime orientation, positioning themselves to fill the commercial void left by the collapse of other trading centers (Gilboa et al. 2008). Archaeological evidence from these sites shows some defensive preparations and signs of stress, but not the complete destruction visible elsewhere. These survivors would play crucial roles in the new world that emerged from the ashes of the Bronze Age system, particularly the Phoenicians, whose maritime trading network and alphabetic writing system would help reconnect the Mediterranean in the centuries that followed. Their resilience demonstrates that collapse, even on this scale, was never total or uniform across the entire region.

Chapter 1

Who Were They? Defining the Enigma

The Sea Peoples in Text and Theory

The term "Sea Peoples" has become a convenient shorthand for the mysterious maritime raiders who appeared in the eastern Mediterranean during the late 13th and early 12th centuries BCE. Yet this designation, so familiar to modern scholars and popular audiences alike, would have been utterly foreign to the ancient peoples who encountered these groups. The phrase "Sea Peoples" is a modern invention, coined in 1881 by the French Egyptologist Gaston Maspero, who used the term peuples de la mer to collectively describe various groups mentioned in Egyptian inscriptions (Sandars 1985; Cline 2014). The ancient Egyptians themselves never used a single umbrella term for these diverse peoples, instead listing specific tribal or ethnic names, sometimes with the qualifier "of the sea" or "from the islands" (Adams and Cohen 2013). Their records, etched in stone and papyrus, speak of individual groups with distinct identities—not a monolithic entity as the modern terminology might suggest.

This modern terminology has contributed to the persistent misconception that the Sea Peoples constituted a unified confederation or migration—a single wave of invaders with a coordinated strategy (Middleton 2017; Sherratt 1998). Archaeological and textual evidence reveals a far more complex reality: multiple groups with distinct material cultures and origins, operating sometimes in concert but often independently, responding to and exacerbating the systemic collapse of Bronze Age Mediterranean civilization (Yasur-Landau 2010; Knapp and Manning 2016). The "Sea Peoples" label has proven useful as a scholarly convention, but it also obscures the diversity and complexity of these populations. Behind this simple designation lies a tapestry of different peoples with varied motivations, cultural practices, and historical trajectories—some seeking conquest, others fleeing disaster, and many simply searching for new lands to settle as their homelands became uninhabitable or politically unstable.

To understand the Sea Peoples phenomenon properly, we must first examine the primary sources that document their activities. These sources are frustratingly limited, with Egyptian inscriptions providing the most detailed accounts, supplemented by fragmentary references in Hittite, Ugaritic, and Cypriote texts (Singer 2000; Pardee 2003). Even these sources present significant interpretive challenges, as they were created not as objective historical records but as political propaganda, religious texts, or desperate communications in times of crisis. The voices of the Sea Peoples themselves remain silent, their stories told only through the perspective of those who fought against them or suffered at their hands. This one-sided narrative has shaped our understanding in ways that may distort the historical reality.

The Egyptian Records: Medinet Habu and the Great Harris Papyrus

The most extensive and detailed account of the Sea Peoples comes from the mortuary temple of Ramesses III at Medinet Habu in Thebes. Built around 1175 BCE, this massive temple complex contains extensive relief carvings and hieroglyphic inscriptions commemorating Ramesses III's military campaigns, including his victories over the Sea Peoples in both land and naval battles (Kitchen 1996; Roberts 2009). The north wall of the temple features a dramatic depiction of a naval engagement, showing Egyptian ships battling against distinctive enemy vessels with bird-head prows and sterns. The accompanying inscriptions describe this as a victory over seaborne invaders who had already devastated other lands. The monumental scale of these reliefs—towering walls covered with intricate carvings—speaks to the significance the Egyptian ruler placed on these victories, presenting them as cosmic triumphs of order over chaos.

The naval battle scene is remarkable for its detail and dynamism. Egyptian warships, identifiable by their lion-head prows and distinctive sail arrangements, engage with enemy vessels in close combat. Egyptian archers fire volleys of arrows while marines board enemy ships. The Sea Peoples' vessels are shown capsizing or already captured, with their crews drowning or surrendering. Egyptian soldiers on shore use bows and javelins against enemy swimmers attempting to reach land. The entire scene conveys the chaos and violence of naval warfare while emphasizing Egyptian military superiority. The carving captures the desperation of the invaders—some flailing in the water, others raising their hands in surrender—contrasted with the disciplined, victorious Egyptian forces. Every detail, from the distinct headdresses of the enemies to the rippling water under the ships, contributes to the narrative of Egyptian triumph over foreign chaos.

The accompanying hieroglyphic text provides crucial information about the identity and origins of these seaborne attackers (Breasted 1906; Kitchen 1996):

"The foreign countries made a conspiracy in their islands. All at once the lands were removed and scattered in the fray. No land could stand before their arms, from Hatti, Kode, Carchemish, Arzawa, and Alashiya on, being cut off at one time. A camp was set up in one place in Amurru. They desolated its people, and its land was like that which has never come into being. They were coming forward toward Egypt, while the flame was prepared before them. Their confederation was the Peleset, Tjekker, Shekelesh, Denyen, and Weshesh, lands united. They laid their hands upon the lands as far as the circuit of the earth, their hearts confident and trusting: 'Our plans will succeed!'"

This text introduces five specific groups—the Peleset, Tjekker, Shekelesh, Denyen, and Weshesh—as participants in a coordinated attack on Egypt. It also establishes a broader context, claiming these groups had already destroyed or damaged other major powers including the Hittite Empire (Hatti), Cyprus (Alashiya), and various states in Syria-Palestine and Anatolia. The description of a camp established in Amurru (the coastal Levant) suggests a staged invasion rather than a single seaborne assault. The inscription paints a picture of unprecedented devastation—lands "scattered in the fray" and desolated "like that which has never come into being"—emphasizing the existential threat these invaders posed not just to Egypt but to the entire established order of the eastern Mediterranean world.

Another wall at Medinet Habu depicts a land battle against the Sea Peoples, showing Egyptian chariots and infantry engaging with enemy warriors (Roberts 2008; Ben-Dor Evian 2016). The Sea Peoples fighters are portrayed with distinctive physical appearances and equipment: some wear horned helmets or feathered headdresses, while others have distinctive hairstyles or headbands. Their weapons include javelins, long and short swords, and round shields. Some fight from two-wheeled carts drawn by oxen, which also appear to transport their women and children—a detail suggesting these were not merely raiders but migrants seeking new lands to settle (Drews 2000; Yasur-Landau 2010). This crucial detail, often overlooked in earlier scholarship, transforms our understanding of the Sea Peoples phenomenon from simple piracy or warfare to a complex population movement involving entire families and communities uprooted from their homelands.

The inscriptions accompanying this land battle scene provide additional context (Kitchen 1996):

"The northern countries quivered in their bodies, namely the Peleset, Tjekker, who were cutting off my land. Their hearts are confident, their plans are fulfilled, so they say. But those who reached my boundary, their seed is not, their heart and their soul are finished forever and ever. As for those who had assembled before them on the sea, the full flame was in their front before the harbor-mouths, and a wall of metal upon the shore surrounded them. They were dragged, overturned, and laid low upon the beach; slain and made heaps from stern to bow of their ships, while all their things were cast upon the water."

This text emphasizes complete Egyptian victory, claiming to have annihilated the invaders both on land and sea. While undoubtedly exaggerated for propagandistic purposes, the detailed descriptions of the battles and enemies suggest a basis in historical events. The mention of women and children traveling with the warriors aligns with archaeological evidence from other sites, indicating population movements rather than simple raiding expeditions (Yasur-Landau 2012). The vivid imagery—enemies "made heaps from stern to bow of their ships" and possessions "cast upon the water"—creates a powerful narrative of total Egyptian dominance, even as it hints at the desperation that might have driven entire peoples to risk such dangerous migrations in search of new homes.

The Great Harris Papyrus, a 41-meter-long document created shortly after Ramesses III's death, provides additional information about his campaigns against the Sea Peoples (Breasted 1906; Wente 1990). It describes the king's preparations to meet the threat:

"I organized my frontier in Zahi [northern Canaan], prepared before them. The princes, commanders of garrisons were stationed as garrison commanders. I caused the river-mouths to be prepared like a strong wall with warships, galleys, and coasters, fully equipped, for they were manned completely from bow to stern with valiant warriors carrying their weapons, and infantry of all the pick of Egypt, being like lions roaring upon the mountains."

The papyrus then describes the outcome of the conflict:

"Those who came forward together on the sea, the full flame was in front of them at the river-mouths, while a stockade of lances surrounded them on the shore. They were dragged ashore, hemmed in, prostrated on the beach, slain, and made into heaps from tail to head. Their ships and their goods were as if fallen into the water."

These accounts from Medinet Habu and the Great Harris Papyrus provide our most detailed information about the Sea Peoples' military encounters with Egypt. However, they represent only one perspective—that of the victorious Egyptians—and must be interpreted with awareness of their propagandistic purpose (Ben-Dor Evian 2017). The texts and images were designed to glorify Ramesses III and demonstrate his fulfillment of the pharaonic duty to maintain cosmic order (ma'at) against the forces of chaos. They tell us more about how the Egyptians wanted to portray these events than about the motivations or origins of the Sea Peoples themselves. The florid language, dramatic imagery, and emphasis on complete victory reflect the conventions of Egyptian royal propaganda rather than objective historical reporting. Reading between the lines, however, we can glimpse the reality of a serious threat that required extraordinary military preparations and resources to counter.

Earlier Encounters: The Merneptah Stele and Ramesses II Records

The confrontations during Ramesses III's reign were not Egypt's first encounters with these maritime groups. The Merneptah Stele, dated to approximately 1208 BCE (about 30 years earlier), records an earlier invasion of the Nile Delta by a coalition that included Libyans and several groups later classified among the Sea Peoples (Kitchen 1996; Redford 1992). This granite monument, discovered in Thebes in 1896, primarily commemorates Pharaoh Merneptah's victory over Libyan invaders, but it also mentions "Ekwesh of the sea," "Teresh of the sea," "Lukka," and "Sherden"—groups that would later be included among the Sea Peoples. The stele stands nearly ten feet tall, its surface covered with hieroglyphic text proclaiming the pharaoh's victories in language both poetic and propagandistic, preserving a crucial earlier chapter in the Sea Peoples narrative.

The stele describes these peoples as allies of the Libyan chief Meryey in an attempted invasion of Egypt (Breasted 1906):

"The wretched, fallen chief of Libya, Meryey son of Ded, has fallen upon the country of Tehenu with his bowmen—Sherden, Shekelesh, Ekwesh, Lukka, Teresh, taking the best of every warrior and every man of war of his country. He has brought his wife and his children... to the western border in the fields of Perire."

The inscription claims a decisive Egyptian victory, with nearly 9,400 enemies killed or captured. Among the spoils listed are distinctive weapons and equipment, including copper swords of the Sherden. This earlier encounter suggests that some Sea Peoples groups were active in the Mediterranean at least a generation before the more famous invasions of the early 12th century BCE (Emanuel 2013). The mention of specific numbers of casualties and captured weapons lends a sense of historical authenticity to the account, though the figures themselves may well be exaggerated. The detail about the Libyan leader bringing "his wife and his children" parallels the later depictions at Medinet Habu, reinforcing the impression that these movements involved entire family groups rather than just warriors.

Even earlier references appear in the records of Ramesses II (r. 1279-1213 BCE), who employed Sherden warriors as mercenaries in his battle against the Hittites at Kadesh around 1274 BCE (Kitchen 1996; Edel 1994). An inscription describes how these Sherden had originally come as enemies:

"His majesty slaughtered and slew them, they being carried off to Egypt, prisoners of his majesty's might, settled in strongholds of the victorious king. He caused the entire land to be united in defending his boundaries. He settled the Sherden whom his sword had taken as captives in strongholds bearing his name."

This practice of incorporating defeated enemies into the Egyptian military continued under Ramesses III, who settled captured Sea Peoples warriors in military colonies (Emanuel 2013). This integration of former enemies into Egyptian society complicates simplistic narratives of invasion and resistance, revealing more complex patterns of conflict, accommodation, and assimilation. The Sherden, initially enemies of Egypt, became valued soldiers in its armies—their distinctive horned helmets and round shields appearing in Egyptian art not just as symbols of defeated foes but as representations of elite troops serving the pharaoh. This transformation from enemy to ally illustrates the fluid nature of identity and allegiance in the late Bronze Age Mediterranean, where pragmatic considerations often trumped ethnic or cultural divisions.

Ugaritic and Hittite Perspectives

While Egyptian sources provide the most detailed accounts of the Sea Peoples, fragmentary texts from other regions offer glimpses of how these maritime groups were perceived elsewhere in the eastern Mediterranean. The kingdom of Ugarit, a wealthy trading center on the Syrian coast, produced several clay tablets mentioning hostile ships and attacks from the sea shortly before its destruction around 1185 BCE (Yon 1992; Singer 1999). These cuneiform tablets, baked hard by the fires that consumed the city, preserve the urgent communications of a kingdom facing imminent destruction—voices from the past speaking directly of fear and desperation in the face of mysterious attackers from the sea.

One particularly poignant letter from the last king of Ugarit to the king of Alashiya (Cyprus) reads (Pardee 2003):

"My father, behold, the enemy's ships came; my cities were burned, and they did evil things in my country. Does not my father know that all my troops and chariots are in the Land of Hatti, and all my ships are in the Land of Lukka? They have not arrived here yet, and the country is thus left to itself... Consider this, my father, there are seven enemy ships that have come and done evil things to me. Now, if there are more enemy ships, let me know about them too, so that I can know."

This desperate communication reveals a kingdom already stripped of its military resources, perhaps due to obligations to its Hittite overlords, facing maritime attackers with insufficient defenses. The letter was never sent—it was found in the ruins of Ugarit's destruction—suggesting the city fell before help could be requested or received. The plaintive tone of the message, with its repeated appeals to "my father" (a formal address between allied rulers) and its admission of vulnerability with troops and ships deployed elsewhere, conveys the helplessness of a once-powerful kingdom facing unexpected attack. The specific mention of "seven enemy ships" provides a rare concrete detail about the scale of at least one Sea Peoples raid—not a massive invasion fleet but a small, perhaps opportunistic attack force that nonetheless proved devastating to a city caught unprepared.

Another Ugaritic tablet reports ships from Shikala (possibly equivalent to the Shekelesh mentioned in Egyptian texts) who "live on boats" and raid coastal settlements (Schaeffer 1968). This characterization of the attackers as primarily maritime people aligns with the Egyptian designation of these groups as "peoples of the sea." The description of people who "live on boats" suggests a truly maritime lifestyle—not just coastal dwellers who occasionally took to the sea, but groups whose primary habitation was aboard their vessels, making them mobile, unpredictable, and difficult to counter through conventional defensive measures. This lifestyle would have made them particularly adaptable to the chaotic conditions of the late Bronze Age collapse, able to move quickly to exploit opportunities or escape threats.

Hittite records also contain scattered references to troublesome coastal raiders (Beckman et al. 2011; Singer 2000). A letter from the last known Hittite king, Suppiluliuma II (c. 1207-1178 BCE), describes a naval battle against ships from Alashiya (Cyprus):

"The ships of the enemy from Alashiya met me in the sea three times for battle, and I destroyed them; I seized the ships and in the midst of the sea I set them on fire."

This rare mention of a Hittite naval victory against maritime enemies comes from the final decades of the Hittite Empire, shortly before its collapse. The identity of these "enemies from Alashiya" remains unclear—they could be Cypriot rebels, Sea Peoples groups using Cyprus as a base, or some other maritime force. What is significant is the evidence of naval warfare in the eastern Mediterranean during precisely the period associated with Sea Peoples activity. The Hittite Empire, traditionally a land power centered in the Anatolian plateau, found itself forced to engage in naval combat—a sign of the changing nature of warfare and threat in this period. The king's boast of setting enemy ships "on fire" in the midst of the sea evokes the dramatic naval battle scenes from Medinet Habu, suggesting similar tactics were employed across the eastern Mediterranean.

Identifying the Sea Peoples: Names and Origins

The Egyptian texts name several distinct groups among the Sea Peoples, providing our primary evidence for their identities. The most frequently mentioned include (Adams and Cohen 2013; Cline and O'Connor 2003):

Peleset (Pw-r-s-t): Widely identified with the biblical Philistines who later settled in the southern coastal plain of Canaan (Dothan 1982; Dothan and Dothan 1992). Archaeological evidence from early Philistine settlements shows strong Aegean cultural influences, suggesting origins in that region (Killebrew 2005; Yasur-Landau 2010). Excavations at sites like Ashdod, Ashkelon, and Ekron have revealed distinctive pottery, architectural features, and cultic items that point to connections with the Aegean world, particularly Mycenaean Greece and Cyprus (Stager 1995; Maeir et al. 2013). The Peleset warriors at Medinet Habu are depicted wearing distinctive feathered headdresses—a style that finds parallels in Aegean art—and carrying unique weapons that set them apart from other groups.

Sherden/Shardana (Š-r-d-n): Possibly connected to Sardinia, though whether as original inhabitants or later migrants remains debated (Vagnetti 2000). They are distinguished in Egyptian art by their horned helmets and round shields, and appear in Egyptian records earlier than other Sea Peoples groups, serving as mercenaries from the time of Ramesses II (Emanuel 2013). Bronze figurines discovered in Sardinia show warriors with similar horned helmets, lending some support to the geographical association. The Sherden appear in Egyptian records spanning over a century, suggesting a long-term relationship that evolved from enmity to military service.

Shekelesh (Š-k-r-š): Often associated with Sicily (classical Sikels), though this identification remains tentative (Vagnetti 2000). They appear in both the Merneptah Stele and the Medinet Habu inscriptions. The linguistic connection between Shekelesh and Sikels is phonetically plausible but difficult to prove conclusively. Archaeological evidence from Sicily during this period shows disruption and cultural change, but direct links to specific Sea Peoples groups remain elusive.

Ekwesh (ꜣ-q-w-š): Frequently identified with the Ahhiyawa mentioned in Hittite texts and possibly the Homeric Achaeans (Greeks) (Beckman et al. 2011; Cline 2009). The Merneptah Stele specifically mentions that the Ekwesh were circumcised, a practice not common among Aegean peoples, which complicates this identification. This curious detail—included perhaps to emphasize the foreignness of these enemies or to document an unusual cultural practice—illustrates the challenges of matching Egyptian designations with known historical groups. If the Ekwesh were indeed Mycenaean Greeks, why would they practice circumcision? This contradiction has led some scholars to question the Achaean identification entirely.

Teresh (T-w-r-š): Sometimes associated with the Tyrrhenians (Etruscans) of western Italy, though this connection remains speculative (Woudhuizen 2006). The Etruscans emerged as a distinct culture in Italy several centuries after the Sea Peoples period, raising questions about the proposed connection. As with many Sea Peoples identifications, the link rests primarily on phonetic similarity between the Egyptian name and the classical ethnonym, a methodology that becomes increasingly problematic as the temporal gap widens.

Tjekker (Ṯ-k-r): Possibly connected to the Teucrians of the Troad (northwestern Anatolia) or to the later city of Dor on the Canaanite coast, where Tjekker settlement is mentioned in the 11th century BCE Egyptian tale of Wenamun (Wente 1990). This later text provides rare evidence for the aftermath of the Sea Peoples invasions, describing a coastal region where former invaders had established permanent settlements and become integrated into the political landscape of the Levant.

Denyen (D-y-n-y): Often identified with the Danuna mentioned in Hittite texts and possibly the Homeric Danaans (Greeks) (Beckman et al. 2011). Some scholars have also suggested connections to the biblical tribe of Dan. The multiple proposed identifications illustrate the challenges of pinpointing the origins of these groups based solely on phonetic similarities in their names.

Weshesh (W-š-š): The least-documented group, with no widely accepted identification. Their inclusion in the Medinet Habu list without further attestation elsewhere highlights the fragmentary nature of our evidence—some groups appear in multiple sources across time, while others are mentioned only once, leaving their identity and role in the broader Sea Peoples phenomenon obscure.

Lukka (R-k): Identified with the inhabitants of southwestern Anatolia, known from Hittite texts as troublesome pirates and raiders (Beckman et al. 2011). The Lukka lands appear in Hittite records spanning centuries before the Sea Peoples period, suggesting a long-established regional identity rather than a newly formed group. Their inclusion among the Sea Peoples illustrates how existing populations could be drawn into the broader patterns of raiding and migration that characterized the period.

These identifications, while commonly cited in both scholarly and popular literature, should be treated with caution. The associations are based primarily on phonetic similarities between the Egyptian names and later ethnonyms known from classical sources—a methodology that is inherently problematic given the limitations of Egyptian hieroglyphic writing for representing foreign names and the centuries-long gap between these texts and classical sources (Yasur-Landau 2003). The Egyptian scribes, working with a writing system not designed to capture the phonetics of Indo-European or Semitic languages, inevitably distorted the original pronunciations, making modern attempts at identification all the more challenging.

The archaeological evidence for these identifications is mixed. The strongest case can be made for the Peleset-Philistine connection, supported by distinctive pottery, architectural features, and burial customs in early Philistine settlements that show clear Aegean influences (Killebrew 1998; Yasur-Landau 2010). For other groups, the material evidence is more ambiguous or entirely lacking. The challenge is further complicated by the likelihood that these were not ethnically homogeneous groups but coalitions formed during the migration process itself, incorporating people from various origins who banded together for survival in a time of crisis.

Early Theories and Persistent Misconceptions

The Sea Peoples captured the imagination of scholars from the moment the Medinet Habu inscriptions were translated in the late 19th century. Early interpretations were heavily influenced by the intellectual currents of their time, particularly the emphasis on migration and invasion as primary drivers of cultural change and the assumption that ethnicity could be directly correlated with material culture (Sandars 1985). The colonial mindset of European archaeology in this period, with its focus on classifying and categorizing peoples and cultures into neat taxonomies, shaped how the Sea Peoples were understood and presented in academic literature.

One of the earliest comprehensive theories was proposed by Gaston Maspero himself, who suggested the Sea Peoples represented a massive migration from the Aegean and western Mediterranean following the Trojan War (Sandars 1985). This theory connected the historical Sea Peoples with Greek mythological traditions, proposing that displaced Achaeans and their allies sought new homes in the eastern Mediterranean after the fall of Troy. The appeal of this theory lay partly in its elegant connection of historical evidence with classical mythology—a synthesis that resonated with 19th-century scholarly approaches that often sought to validate ancient literary traditions through archaeological evidence.

In the early 20th century, scholars like Eduard Meyer and John Garstang developed more nuanced interpretations but still emphasized large-scale migration as the primary explanation (Drews 1993). The discovery of widespread destruction layers at Late Bronze Age sites across the eastern Mediterranean seemed to provide archaeological confirmation of the devastating invasions described in the Egyptian texts. As excavations revealed burnt palaces, abandoned cities, and cultural disruption spanning from Greece to the Levant, the Sea Peoples emerged as convenient agents of destruction—a single explanation for a complex pattern of collapse.

By the mid-20th century, a standard narrative had emerged: the Sea Peoples were primarily Aegean and western Mediterranean peoples displaced by upheavals in their homelands, who moved eastward as a massive migration/invasion force, destroying the Hittite Empire and numerous other centers before being repulsed by Egypt (Sandars 1985; Drews 1993). Some scholars, like Rhys Carpenter, connected this migration to climate events, suggesting prolonged drought in the Aegean had triggered the population movements. This environmental determinism offered a compelling causal mechanism, though it tended to oversimplify the complex interactions between climate, society, politics, and culture that shape human responses to environmental stress.

This traditional narrative persists in popular accounts and some academic works, but it has been increasingly challenged by archaeological evidence and more critical readings of the textual sources (Sherratt 1998; Yasur-Landau 2010; Middleton 2017). Several persistent misconceptions continue to shape public understanding of the Sea Peoples:

The unified confederation fallacy: The Egyptian texts, particularly at Medinet Habu, describe multiple groups acting in concert against Egypt. This has led to the misconception that the Sea Peoples constituted a unified confederation with coordinated strategies across the Mediterranean (Sherratt 1998). Archaeological evidence suggests a much more complex reality, with different groups operating independently in different regions, sometimes in conflict with each other. The apparent coordination described in Egyptian sources likely reflects specific alliances formed for particular campaigns rather than a pan-Mediterranean confederation with centralized leadership.

The pure invasion model: While the Egyptian texts emphasize military confrontations, they also contain hints that the Sea Peoples included civilian populations seeking new lands to settle (Drews 2000; Yasur-Landau 2010). The depiction of families traveling in ox-carts at Medinet Habu suggests population movement rather than purely military expeditions. Modern scholarship increasingly views the Sea Peoples phenomenon as a complex mixture of raiding, migration, and opportunistic settlement in destabilized regions. Some groups may have begun as refugees fleeing collapse in their homelands, only turning to raiding out of desperation. Others may have been opportunistic predators exploiting the weakening of established powers. Most likely combined elements of both, adapting their strategies to changing circumstances.

The single cause assumption: Earlier scholarship often sought a single trigger for the Sea Peoples movements—whether Aegean drought, political collapse, or technological change (Drews 1993). Current approaches emphasize multiple interacting factors, including climate change, resource depletion, political instability, and changing patterns of trade and warfare (Knapp and Manning 2016; Kaniewski et al. 2013). The complex systems that supported Bronze Age civilization were vulnerable to cascading failures, where disruption in one sector—trade routes, agricultural production, palatial administration—could trigger wider instability. The Sea Peoples may be better understood as both symptoms and agents of this systemic crisis than as its primary cause.

The exclusive focus on textual identifications: The effort to match the groups named in Egyptian texts with known historical peoples has sometimes overshadowed archaeological approaches to understanding the material culture and actual movements of populations during this period (Yasur-Landau 2003; Middleton 2017). The archaeological evidence reveals complex patterns of continuity and disruption that do not always align neatly with the narrative suggested by the texts. Material culture changes—new pottery styles, burial practices, architectural techniques—provide evidence for population movements that may correspond to Sea Peoples activity, but these changes rarely map cleanly onto the ethnic labels provided by Egyptian sources.

Recent scholarship has moved toward more nuanced interpretations that integrate textual and archaeological evidence while acknowledging the limitations of both (Oren 2000; Killebrew and Lehmann 2013). The Sea Peoples are increasingly viewed not as external invaders who caused the Bronze Age collapse, but as both products and agents of a systemic crisis that affected the entire eastern Mediterranean world (Sherratt 1998; Middleton 2017). Their activities accelerated existing patterns of instability, creating feedback loops that ultimately transformed the political and cultural landscape of the region. This perspective shifts focus from identifying specific ethnic groups to understanding the complex processes of migration, adaptation, and cultural change that characterized this pivotal period in Mediterranean history.

Chapter 2

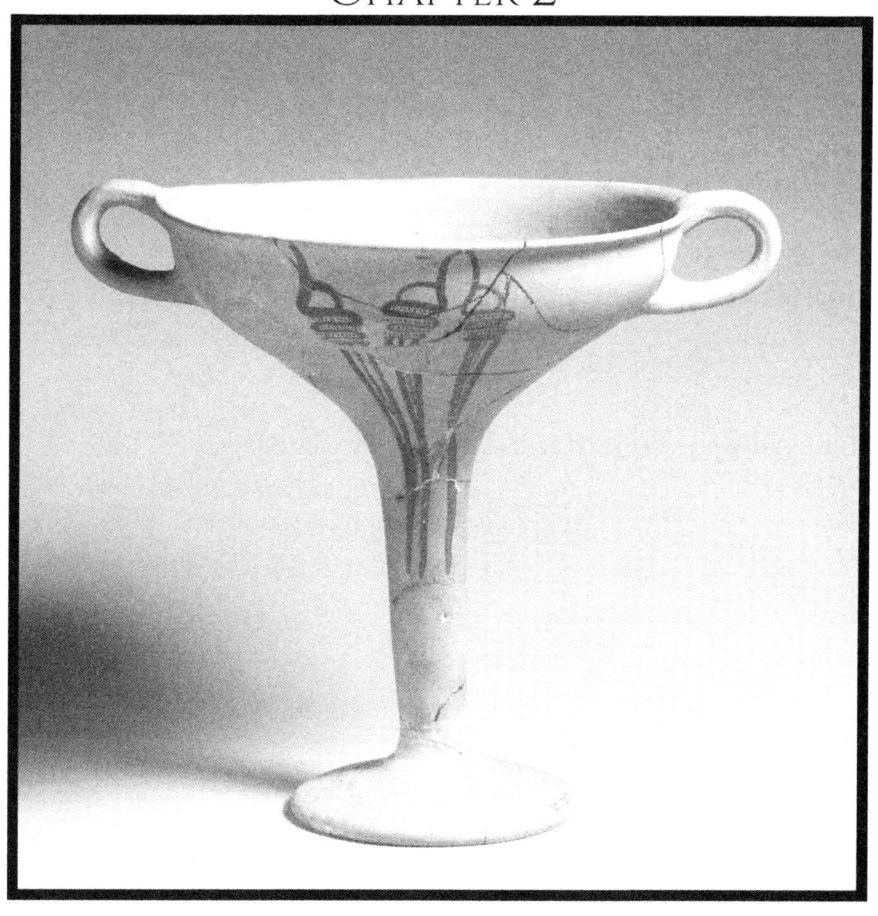

The First Waves: Early Incursions

Early Appearances: The Sea Peoples Before the Crisis

While the dramatic naval and land battles depicted at Medinet Habu represent the most extensive visual and textual evidence for the Sea Peoples, these groups did not suddenly materialize in the early 12th century BCE. Egyptian records document encounters with several of these maritime peoples decades—and in some cases centuries—before the crisis that brought down the Bronze Age system. These earlier attestations provide crucial context for understanding the evolving relationship between Egypt and these groups, suggesting a more complex dynamic than simple invasion narratives imply.

The Sherden: From Raiders to Royal Guards

Among the Sea Peoples groups, the Sherden (also transcribed as Shardana or Šrdn) have the longest documented history of interaction with Egypt. Their first appearance in Egyptian texts dates to the Amarna period (14th century BCE), where they are mentioned in EA 81, a letter from the king of Byblos to the Egyptian pharaoh, describing "Šerdanu men of the king" who had killed a nobleman (Moran 1992: 151). This reference suggests that already by the mid-14th century BCE, some Sherden were serving as mercenaries or guards in Egyptian-controlled territories in the Levant.

More substantial evidence comes from the reign of Ramesses II (1279-1213 BCE). The Tanis Stele II, dating to approximately the second year of his reign (c. 1277 BCE), describes an encounter with Sherden raiders:

"The mighty arm of Pharaoh captured the Sherden who came as enemies, sailing in their warships from the midst of the Great Green (the Mediterranean), and none were able to stand before them" (Kitchen 1996: 119-120).

The text goes on to describe how these captured Sherden were subsequently incorporated into the Egyptian military:

"Now they are brought captive to Egypt, as numerous as the sand of the shore. I have placed them in strongholds bearing my name, made into companies and battalions like the soldiers of Egypt" (Kitchen 1996: 120).

This pattern—capturing raiders and converting them into military assets—appears to have been a deliberate Egyptian strategy for dealing with these maritime threats. By the time of the Battle of Kadesh (c. 1274 BCE), fought against the Hittites in Syria, the Sherden were serving as an elite personal guard for Ramesses II. The Kadesh inscriptions specifically mention "the Sherden of His Majesty's capturing" as part of the pharaoh's bodyguard (Kitchen 1996: 21), indicating that these former enemies had been integrated into the highest echelons of the Egyptian military hierarchy.

Visual evidence for the Sherden's distinctive appearance comes from multiple sources. At Abu Simbel, reliefs depicting the Battle of Kadesh show Sherden warriors with their characteristic horned helmets (often with a disk between the horns), round shields, and long swords fighting alongside Egyptian forces (Darnell & Manassa 2007: 87-89). Similar depictions appear at the Ramesseum in Thebes and at Abydos. These visual representations allow us to track the Sherden's continued presence in Egyptian military service through multiple campaigns of Ramesses II's reign.

The archaeological correlates for the Sherden remain contested. Many scholars have suggested connections to Sardinia, noting both the phonetic similarity between "Sherden" and "Sardinia" and the presence of bronze figurines on Sardinia depicting warriors with horned helmets (Lo Schiavo 2005: 400-402). Others have proposed links to sites in northern Syria, Cyprus, or the Aegean. Recent strontium isotope analysis of skeletal remains from potential "Sea Peoples" settlements in the Levant may eventually provide more definitive evidence for their geographic origins (Yasur-Landau 2010: 114-116).

What is clear from the Egyptian evidence is that the Sherden maintained a complex relationship with Egypt for at least a century before the major Sea Peoples conflicts of the early 12th century BCE. They appear to have transitioned from occasional raiders to valued mercenaries, demonstrating both the permeability of ethnic and political boundaries in the Late Bronze Age and Egypt's pragmatic approach to managing potential threats.

The Lukka: Anatolian Raiders

Another group with a long history of interaction with Egypt were the Lukka (or Luka), generally associated with southwest Anatolia, specifically the classical region of Lycia. Unlike the Sherden, who appear to have originated from more distant shores, the Lukka were a recognized territorial entity within the broader Near Eastern diplomatic world.

The earliest Egyptian reference to the Lukka appears in the Annals of Thutmose III (c. 1479-1425 BCE), where they are listed among peoples who brought tribute to Egypt (Redford 2003: 65). However, their relationship with Egypt and other major powers was often antagonistic. Hittite texts from the 14th-13th centuries BCE repeatedly mention the Lukka lands as a troublesome region on their southwestern frontier, often in rebellion or conducting raids against Hittite territory (Bryce 2005: 132-134).

The most substantial Egyptian reference to Lukka aggression comes from the Amarna letters, specifically EA 38, a letter from the king of Alashiya (Cyprus) to the Egyptian pharaoh, dating to the mid-14th century BCE:

"As to the matter of the Lukka, about which you wrote to me, I know nothing of their seizing a village in your land. I am herewith writing to you so that you may know this. But if people from my land have done wrong, you yourself do what is appropriate" (Moran 1992: 111).

This letter indicates that the Lukka were engaged in maritime raiding activities that affected Egyptian interests, with their attacks extending as far as Egyptian-controlled territories. The king of Alashiya's careful diplomatic language suggests both the seriousness of these raids and the complex jurisdictional issues they raised in the interconnected Late Bronze Age world.

By the reign of Ramesses II, the Lukka appear among Egypt's enemies at the Battle of Kadesh, fighting alongside the Hittites as part of a coalition of Anatolian states (Kitchen 1996: 27). Later, during the reign of Merneptah (c. 1213-1203 BCE), they are listed among the Sea Peoples coalition that attacked Egypt, appearing alongside the Sherden, Ekwesh, Teresh, and Shekelesh (Manassa 2003: 54-55).

Archaeological evidence potentially connecting material culture to the textual references to the Lukka remains limited. However, survey work in southwest Anatolia has identified settlement patterns and ceramic assemblages that may correspond to the Lukka lands mentioned in Hittite texts (Vanhaverbeke & Waelkens 2003: 225-228). The coastal orientation of many Late Bronze Age sites in this region aligns with the maritime activities attributed to the Lukka in textual sources.

The Lukka appear to have maintained their identity into the Early Iron Age, potentially evolving into the classical Lycians known from Greek and Persian sources. Their longevity as a regional entity distinguishes them from some other Sea Peoples groups and suggests they may represent a different phenomenon—an established Anatolian population that opportunistically expanded their raiding activities during the turbulent final decades of the Bronze Age rather than a displaced migrant group.

The Ekwesh and the Question of Aegean Origins

The Ekwesh (also transcribed as Akaiwasha or Eqwesh) present one of the most intriguing cases among the early-attested Sea Peoples groups due to their potential connection to the Ahhiyawa mentioned in Hittite texts and, by extension, to the Achaeans (Mycenaean Greeks) known from Homeric tradition.

Their primary appearance in Egyptian records comes from the Great Karnak Inscription of Merneptah, dating to approximately 1208 BCE, which describes an invasion of Libya that included Sea Peoples allies:

"The wretched, fallen chief of Libya, Meryey son of Ded, has fallen upon the country of Tehenu with his bowmen—Sherden, Shekelesh, Ekwesh, Lukka, Teresh, taking the best of every warrior and every man of war of his country. He has brought his wife and his children... leading the captains of war in front of him, to fall upon the land of Egypt" (Manassa 2003: 55).

What makes the Ekwesh particularly noteworthy is an additional detail provided in the inscription: they are described as being "of the countries of the sea" and, uniquely among the groups listed, as being "foreskinned" (Redford 1992: 246). This latter detail has been interpreted as indicating that, unlike the circumcised Egyptians and many Near Eastern peoples, the Ekwesh practiced no circumcision—a cultural trait consistent with Aegean populations.

The potential identification of the Ekwesh with Mycenaean Greeks remains debated. The phonetic similarity between Ekwesh/Akaiwasha and Ahhiyawa/Achaeans is suggestive but not conclusive. If correct, however, this identification would have significant implications for understanding the collapse of Mycenaean civilization and the movements of Aegean populations during the late 13th century BCE.

Archaeological evidence for Mycenaean decline during this period is substantial. Between approximately 1250-1200 BCE, major palatial centers across mainland Greece were destroyed, including Mycenae, Tiryns, Pylos, and Thebes (Middleton 2020: 87-89). While local factors likely played important roles in these destructions, the rough synchronicity of collapse across widely separated regions suggests broader systemic pressures.

If some displaced Mycenaeans did indeed participate in the Libyan invasion described by Merneptah, it would indicate that Aegean population movements were already underway several decades before the more famous Sea Peoples conflicts of the early 12th century BCE. This earlier dating challenges simplified narratives that place all Sea Peoples activity within a narrow chronological window and suggests a more prolonged period of increasing instability.

The Shekelesh and Teresh: Western Mediterranean Connections?

The Shekelesh (or Sheklesh) and Teresh (or Tursha) frequently appear together in Egyptian texts, beginning with Merneptah's records of the Libyan campaign and continuing through the Ramesses III inscriptions. Both groups have been tentatively connected to western Mediterranean origins based on phonetic similarities: Shekelesh with Sicily/Sicels and Teresh with Tyrrhenians (Etruscans).

In the fifth year of Merneptah's reign (c. 1208 BCE), both groups participated in the Libyan invasion of Egypt as mercenaries or allies of the Libyan chief Meryey. The Great Karnak Inscription describes their defeat:

"The Shekelesh and Teresh were destroyed, their seed is not... Their hearts are removed, taken away, and their soul is wasted" (Manassa 2003: 56).

Despite this claimed annihilation, both groups reappear approximately 30 years later among the Sea Peoples coalition confronting Ramesses III, suggesting either that the earlier defeat was exaggerated or that these ethnic labels represented broader populations than those specifically engaged in the Libyan campaign.

Material evidence potentially connecting these textual references to archaeological cultures remains limited. The traditional association of the Shekelesh with Sicily is supported primarily by the phonetic similarity to the Sicels mentioned in later classical sources rather than by direct archaeological connections (Broodbank 2013: 461-463). Similarly, the proposed link between the Teresh and proto-Etruscans relies more on linguistic arguments than clear material culture correlations.

Recent archaeological work in Sicily has identified evidence of disruption and population movement during the late 13th and early 12th centuries BCE, including the abandonment of some coastal sites and changes in material culture (Leighton 1999: 172-175). However, connecting these changes specifically to the Shekelesh mentioned in Egyptian texts remains speculative.

What the Egyptian sources do clearly indicate is that both groups were engaged in maritime activities across significant distances by the late 13th century BCE, with at least some elements operating as mercenaries or raiders along the North African coast. Their repeated appearances in Egyptian records spanning several decades suggest persistent interaction rather than a single migration event.

Patterns of Interaction: Raiders, Mercenaries, and Migrants

The various Sea Peoples groups documented in Egyptian sources prior to the major conflicts of the early 12th century BCE demonstrate several distinct patterns of interaction with Egypt and other eastern Mediterranean powers. These patterns help illuminate the complex role these groups played in Late Bronze Age geopolitics and challenge simplistic characterizations of them as either pure invaders or homogeneous refugees.

Maritime Raiding as Economic Strategy

The consistent Egyptian characterization of groups like the Sherden and Lukka as maritime raiders reflects a widespread economic strategy in the Late Bronze Age Mediterranean. Naval raiding represented a form of resource acquisition that operated alongside, and sometimes in competition with, more formal trade networks.

Maritime raiding in this period should not be understood through the anachronistic lens of later piracy. Rather, it often represented a legitimate, if contested, form of resource acquisition for communities with limited agricultural land or other resources. The distinction between raiding and trading was frequently situational rather than absolute, with the same groups engaging in peaceful exchange in some contexts and forceful appropriation in others (Hitchcock & Maeir 2014: 624-625).

The geography of the eastern Mediterranean, with its numerous islands, peninsulas, and sheltered harbors, created ideal conditions for such raiding economies to develop. Communities with maritime expertise could exploit the rich trade networks of the Late Bronze Age, targeting vulnerable merchant vessels or coastal settlements. The valuable cargo carried by ships like the Uluburun vessel, with its tons of copper ingots, glass, ivory, and luxury goods, presented tempting targets (Pulak 1998: 215-218).

Egyptian responses to these raids evolved over time. Initial encounters typically involved military confrontation, as described in the Tanis Stele regarding the Sherden. However, Egypt's longer-term strategy often focused on co-option rather than elimination, converting former raiders into mercenaries or settled subjects. This pattern reflects both pragmatic military considerations—utilizing the fighting skills of these groups—and a broader Egyptian approach to incorporating foreign populations into their imperial system.

Mercenary Service and Military Mobility

The transition from raiders to mercenaries documented for the Sherden highlights another key aspect of Sea Peoples identity: their role as military specialists in multiple eastern Mediterranean armies. This military mobility created complex, shifting allegiances that transcended simple ethnic or geographic categorizations.

By the late 13th century BCE, Sea Peoples mercenaries are documented serving not only in Egyptian forces but also in Hittite armies and alongside Libyan chiefs. The Hittite king Hattusili III (c. 1267-1237 BCE) mentions "Sherden of the sea" in correspondence with the king of Ugarit, suggesting their presence in Syrian coastal regions under Hittite influence (Singer 1999: 729). This widespread distribution indicates that these groups possessed military skills valued across multiple political systems.

The specific martial abilities that made Sea Peoples warriors desirable as mercenaries likely included naval expertise, familiarity with certain weapons systems, and possibly forms of combat training or tactics distinct from those of Near Eastern armies. Egyptian depictions consistently show the Sherden armed with distinctive equipment—horned helmets, round shields, and long swords—suggesting they maintained their traditional fighting methods even when serving under Egyptian command (Darnell & Manassa 2007: 88).

This pattern of mercenary service had significant implications for the later Sea Peoples conflicts. Warriors who had served in Egyptian or Hittite armies would have gained intimate knowledge of these empires' military systems, defensive infrastructure, and territorial vulnerabilities. When political or environmental pressures later led these groups to act against their former employers, they could exploit this insider knowledge to devastating effect.

The mercenary experience also facilitated cultural exchange and hybridization. Sea Peoples who served in Egyptian garrisons or Hittite border forces would have been exposed to the languages, religious practices, and material culture of these societies, potentially adopting elements that they later carried with them during subsequent migrations. This process may help explain the mixed cultural assemblages often associated with Sea Peoples settlements in the Levant during the Early Iron Age.

From Raiders to Migrants: The Demographic Question

Perhaps the most significant shift in Sea Peoples activity between the earlier attestations and the major conflicts of the early 12th century BCE involves scale and intent. The earlier encounters documented during the reigns of Ramesses II and Merneptah primarily involved military engagements with warrior groups, while the later conflicts described by Ramesses III appear to have included significant civilian populations seeking territory for settlement.

The reliefs at Medinet Habu explicitly depict non-combatants among the Sea Peoples forces that attacked Egypt around 1175 BCE:

"The foreign countries made a conspiracy in their islands... Their main support was Peleset, Tjekker, Shekelesh, Denyen, and Wesheh, lands united. They laid their hands upon the lands to the very circuit of the earth... They were coming forward toward Egypt, while the flame was prepared before them. Their confederation was the Peleset, Tjekker, Shekelesh, Denyen, and Weshesh, united lands. They laid their hands upon the countries as far as the circuit of the earth, their hearts confident and trusting: 'Our plans will succeed!'" (Wilson 1969: 262).

Accompanying these texts, the reliefs show ox-carts carrying women and children alongside the warriors (O'Connor 2000: 94-95). This evidence suggests a fundamental transformation in the nature of Sea Peoples activity—from primarily military raiding and mercenary service to a more complex phenomenon involving population displacement and territorial acquisition.

This shift raises important questions about the demographic scale of Sea Peoples movements. Were these mass migrations involving entire ethnic groups, or more limited population movements involving specific segments of society? The archaeological evidence suggests considerable variation, with some regions experiencing wholesale population replacement while others show more limited infiltration or elite dominance (Yasur-Landau 2010: 216-220).

The factors driving this transformation from raiding to migration likely included both push factors (environmental stress, political collapse, resource depletion in home territories) and pull factors (knowledge of vulnerable territories, existing diaspora communities established through earlier mercenary service). The timing of this shift—occurring during a period of widespread systems collapse across the eastern Mediterranean—suggests that the Sea Peoples were responding to the same pressures that affected the broader Bronze Age world rather than simply causing them.

Beyond Raiders and Invaders: Rethinking Sea Peoples Identity

The documented interactions between Egypt and various Sea Peoples groups during the decades preceding the Bronze Age collapse suggest we need a more nuanced understanding of who these people were and how they related to the broader Mediterranean world. Rather than seeing them as external invaders who suddenly appeared to destroy Bronze Age civilization, the evidence points to groups with long-standing connections to the eastern Mediterranean who adapted their strategies in response to changing conditions.

Hybrid Identities and Flexible Allegiances

The complex patterns of interaction documented in Egyptian sources—with groups like the Sherden transitioning from enemies to valued mercenaries, or the Lukka alternating between tribute-bearers and raiders—suggest that Sea Peoples identities were fluid and situational rather than fixed. These groups appear to have maintained distinctive cultural markers (as evidenced by their consistent depiction with characteristic weapons and dress in Egyptian art) while simultaneously adapting to new political contexts.

This flexibility extended to political allegiances. The same groups that fought against Egypt under Merneptah later attacked Egypt under Ramesses III, while others, like elements of the Sherden, apparently remained loyal to Egypt even as their ethnic kin joined the invading forces. These shifting alliances suggest that "Sea Peoples" identity was not primarily defined by opposition to established powers but rather by other factors—perhaps maritime expertise, certain cultural practices, or forms of social organization—that transcended immediate political affiliations.

The hybrid nature of Sea Peoples identity is further suggested by archaeological evidence from sites associated with their settlement after the Bronze Age collapse. At locations like Tell Tayinat and Tell Miqne (Ekron) in the Levant, material culture shows a mixture of Aegean, Cypriot, Anatolian, and local Canaanite elements rather than a single, clearly defined cultural package (Killebrew 2005: 230-233). This hybridity suggests that the groups collectively labeled as "Sea Peoples" by the Egyptians may themselves have been multicultural coalitions rather than homogeneous ethnic units.

Maritime Networks and Connectivity

The consistent association of Sea Peoples groups with maritime activity—whether raiding, mercenary service, or eventual migration—highlights the importance of Mediterranean connectivity in shaping their identity and activities. Rather than viewing them primarily as terrestrial populations who occasionally took to the sea, we should perhaps understand them as fundamentally maritime communities whose lifeways were centered on sea-based movement and exchange.

This maritime orientation would have given these groups distinct advantages during the turbulent final decades of the Bronze Age. As land-based trade routes became disrupted by political instability or conflict, maritime communities could maintain connections across the Mediterranean, accessing resources and information that became increasingly inaccessible to palace-centered states. Their mobility also provided a crucial adaptive advantage, allowing them to relocate in response to environmental or political pressures rather than being tied to specific territories.

Recent archaeological research has increasingly emphasized the role of maritime networks in facilitating cultural exchange and population movement throughout Mediterranean prehistory (Broodbank 2013: 431-436). The Sea Peoples may represent a particularly visible manifestation of these long-standing networks during a period when the breakdown of palatial systems made such alternative forms of social organization and resource acquisition increasingly viable.

Economic Opportunism and Adaptation

The evolving patterns of Sea Peoples activity documented in Egyptian sources—from raiding to mercenary service to territorial acquisition—can be understood as strategic adaptations to changing economic conditions in the late 13th and early 12th centuries BCE. As the integrated Bronze Age economy began to fragment, groups with maritime expertise and military skills exploited emerging opportunities while adapting to new constraints.

Initial raiding activities targeted the wealth generated by the palace-centered trade systems, extracting resources from the existing economic order. Mercenary service represented another strategy for accessing these resources, exchanging military expertise for wealth and status within the established political systems. When these systems began to collapse, territorial acquisition offered a means of securing more direct control over agricultural land and trade routes, providing a more sustainable economic base in an increasingly destabilized world.

This pattern of opportunistic adaptation suggests that the Sea Peoples were not simply reactionary forces opposing Bronze Age civilization but active participants in the complex processes of systems transformation that characterized this period. Their activities both responded to and accelerated the breakdown of palatial economies, contributing to the emergence of new, more decentralized forms of economic and political organization that would characterize the early Iron Age.

Implications for Understanding the Bronze Age Collapse

Recognizing the long history of interaction between Egypt and various Sea Peoples groups before the major conflicts of the early 12th century BCE has important implications for how we understand their role in the broader Bronze Age collapse. Rather than seeing them as an external force that suddenly appeared to destroy established civilizations, we should view them as integral components of the Late Bronze Age Mediterranean system who both responded to and contributed to its transformation.

From External Shock to System Transformation

The traditional narrative of the Bronze Age collapse often positioned the Sea Peoples as an external shock—a sudden, unexpected force that overwhelmed otherwise stable civilizations. The evidence for decades of prior interaction between these groups and the major powers of the eastern Mediterranean challenges this framing. The Sea Peoples were not external to the Bronze Age system but embedded within it, operating along its maritime frontiers and occasionally penetrating its core through mercenary service or raiding.

Their transformation from periodic raiders and military specialists to territorial competitors occurred within the context of broader systemic stresses affecting the entire eastern Mediterranean. Climate data from multiple sources indicates that the period between approximately 1250-1150 BCE experienced significant aridity in the eastern Mediterranean region, potentially disrupting agricultural production in marginal areas (Drake 2012: 1862-1870; Kaniewski et al. 2013: 9-12). Simultaneously, archaeological evidence documents disruptions to trade networks, abandonment of settlements, and increased fortification construction across multiple regions (Knapp & Manning 2016: 99-120).

Within this context, the activities of Sea Peoples groups—whether raiding, mercenary service, or eventual migration—represent adaptations to changing conditions rather than exogenous shocks. Their maritime mobility and military expertise became increasingly valuable assets in a destabilizing world, allowing them to exploit vulnerabilities in the palace-centered states while pursuing alternative strategies for resource acquisition.

Cascading Failures and Feedback Loops

Understanding the Sea Peoples as components of the Bronze Age system rather than external invaders allows us to better appreciate the complex dynamics of the collapse process. The integrated nature of Late Bronze Age societies—with their interconnected trade networks, diplomatic relations, and resource dependencies—created conditions where disruption in one area could trigger cascading failures across the broader system.

Sea Peoples activities likely contributed to these cascading failures through several mechanisms:

These disruptions would have created feedback loops, where initial system stresses led to responses that generated new stresses, accelerating the process of transformation. For example, the diversion of resources to military defense might have undermined agricultural production or maintenance of trade infrastructure, further weakening economic systems and creating new vulnerabilities that maritime raiders could exploit.

Victims and Agents of Collapse

Perhaps most significantly, the long history of Sea Peoples activity before the final Bronze Age collapse suggests that these groups were both victims and agents of the broader system transformation. The same environmental, economic, and political pressures that destabilized palace-centered states also affected maritime communities, forcing them to adapt their strategies for survival and resource acquisition.

Some Sea Peoples groups—particularly those potentially connected to the Aegean, like the Ekwesh—may have been displaced by the collapse of Mycenaean palatial centers, making them refugees seeking new territories. Others, like the Lukka, appear to have expanded their traditional raiding activities in response to new opportunities created by the weakening of major powers. Still others, like elements of the Sherden, maintained their positions within surviving power structures like the Egyptian military while their ethnic kin joined opposing forces.

This diversity of experiences and strategies cautions against monolithic characterizations of the Sea Peoples as either simple destroyers or innocent refugees. They were active participants in a complex process of system transformation, making strategic decisions in response to changing conditions while simultaneously contributing to those changes through their actions.

Conclusion: Beyond the "Invasion" Narrative

The extensive evidence for Sea Peoples activity in the eastern Mediterranean prior to the major conflicts of the early 12th century BCE demonstrates the inadequacy of simple "invasion" narratives for understanding their role in the Bronze Age collapse. These groups had long-standing relationships with Egypt and other major powers, operating variously as raiders, mercenaries, trading partners, and eventually territorial competitors over many decades.

Their transformation from periodic maritime threats to significant political actors capable of challenging major powers like Egypt reflects broader processes of system transformation that affected the entire eastern Mediterranean during the late 13th and early 12th centuries BCE. Climate change, resource pressures, political instability, and shifts in patterns of trade and warfare created conditions where maritime mobility and military expertise became increasingly valuable assets, allowing Sea Peoples groups to exploit emerging opportunities while adapting to new constraints.

Rather than viewing the Sea Peoples as external invaders who destroyed Bronze Age civilization, we should understand them as integral components of a complex adaptive system undergoing rapid transformation. Their activities both responded to and contributed to this transformation, helping to shape the new political and cultural landscape that emerged in the early Iron Age.

This perspective shifts our focus from questions of ethnic identification and invasion routes to more nuanced considerations of how different groups navigated the challenges and opportunities presented by systemic collapse. The Sea Peoples were neither simple destroyers nor passive victims but active participants in one of the most significant periods of cultural and political transformation in Mediterranean history.

Chapter 3

The Great Cataclysm: The Reign of Ramesses III

Medinet Habu and the Sea Peoples Crisis

The most comprehensive visual and textual record of the Sea Peoples conflict comes from the mortuary temple of Ramesses III at Medinet Habu, located on the west bank of the Nile opposite Thebes in Upper Egypt. Constructed between approximately 1186 and 1155 BCE, this massive complex served not only as a funerary monument but as a powerful propaganda statement asserting Ramesses III's legitimacy through military victory (Kitchen 1996). The temple walls preserve an extraordinary visual narrative of Egypt's confrontation with the Sea Peoples, complemented by extensive hieroglyphic inscriptions that provide crucial context for understanding this pivotal moment in Mediterranean history.

"The Medinet Habu reliefs represent our most detailed visual source for understanding the nature of Sea Peoples warfare and their distinctive material culture," wrote Egyptologist Nancy Sandars in her seminal work on the subject. "No other Bronze Age monument provides such a comprehensive depiction of naval combat from this period" (Sandars 1985: 127).

The Temple Context: Monumental Propaganda

The mortuary temple itself stands as a testament to Egyptian royal ideology during a period of existential threat. Modeled after the nearby Ramesseum of Ramesses II, Medinet Habu's architectural program follows established conventions while introducing distinctive elements that reflect the specific challenges of Ramesses III's reign (Shaw 2000). The temple complex, enclosed by massive mud-brick walls with stone-faced gates modeled after Syrian fortresses, creates a microcosm of Egypt's defended borders—a physical manifestation of the pharaoh's role as protector of the Two Lands.

The Sea Peoples reliefs appear prominently on the exterior north wall of the main temple structure, where they would be visible to visitors approaching from the entrance pylon. Their placement alongside scenes depicting campaigns against the Libyans and Nubians follows the conventional Egyptian practice of representing the pharaoh's victories over the traditional enemies from all cardinal directions (Redford 1992). However, the unprecedented scale and detail devoted to the Sea Peoples conflict underscores its exceptional importance in Ramesses III's reign.

"The prominence given to these scenes reflects not merely conventional pharaonic boasting," observed Egyptologist James Weinstein, "but the genuine existential threat that the Sea Peoples invasion represented to the Egyptian state during this period of broader regional collapse" (Weinstein 1992: 145).

The Naval Battle: Unprecedented Maritime Warfare

The most innovative and historically significant section of the Medinet Habu reliefs depicts what may be the earliest detailed representation of a naval battle in art history. Located on the north exterior wall, these scenes show the Egyptian fleet engaging the Sea Peoples ships in the waters of what the accompanying text identifies as "the mouth of the Nile" (Breasted 1906, Vol. 4: 37-89). The battle unfolds across several registers, with Egyptian and Sea Peoples vessels locked in deadly combat.

The Sea Peoples ships display distinctive features that set them apart from Egyptian vessels. While Egyptian ships feature papyriform prows and sterns (curved ends resembling papyrus plants), the enemy vessels have high, curved stems terminating in bird-head devices—a design consistent with Aegean and Eastern Mediterranean shipbuilding traditions (Wachsmann 1998). Each Sea Peoples ship carries multiple warriors, depicted with their distinctive headgear and weapons.

The accompanying inscription provides Ramesses III's version of events:

"Those who came forward together on the sea, the full flame was in front of them at the river-mouths, while a stockade of lances surrounded them on the shore. They were dragged in, enclosed, and prostrated on the beach, killed, and made into heaps from tail to head. Their ships and their goods were as if fallen into the water" (Kitchen 1996: 15).

This dramatic account suggests a coordinated Egyptian strategy: luring the Sea Peoples fleet into the confined waters of a Nile branch where they could be trapped between Egyptian ships and troops stationed on the shoreline. The relief images support this interpretation, showing Egyptian archers firing from both ships and the riverbank while Sea Peoples warriors fall into the water.

Particularly notable in these scenes is the advanced naval warfare technology displayed by both sides. The Egyptian ships feature both rowers and sails, giving them tactical flexibility, while Egyptian marines employ a mix of ranged and close-combat weapons. Some Egyptian vessels appear to be equipped with crow's nest platforms from which archers can fire down onto enemy ships. The Sea Peoples rely primarily on warriors armed for hand-to-hand combat, suggesting a strategy focused on boarding and capturing enemy vessels rather than sinking them.

"The naval battle scenes at Medinet Habu provide unprecedented insight into Bronze Age maritime combat tactics," noted maritime archaeologist Shelley Wachsmann. "They suggest that the Sea Peoples had developed specialized naval forces capable of challenging even Egypt, the most powerful remaining Bronze Age state, on the water" (Wachsmann 1998: 211).

The Land Battle: Clash of Military Systems

Adjacent to the naval battle scenes, the Medinet Habu reliefs depict a massive land engagement between Egyptian forces and the Sea Peoples (Roberts 2009). These reliefs portray the Sea Peoples as a mixed force of infantry and chariotry, advancing in organized formations against the Egyptian army led personally by Ramesses III in his chariot.

The land battle scenes emphasize several key aspects of the conflict:

Distinctive Sea Peoples Material Culture: The reliefs meticulously depict the Sea Peoples warriors with characteristic features that distinguish different groups. Most notable are their unique headdresses: some wear horned helmets (associated with the Sherden), others display distinctive "feathered" or reed headdresses (identified with the Peleset), and still others wear caps or headbands (Dothan 1982). Their weapons and armor also receive careful attention, with many warriors carrying round shields, long spears, and straight swords distinct from Egyptian military equipment.

Mixed Military Forces: The Sea Peoples are shown employing both infantry formations and ox-drawn carts carrying warriors and their families. These are not typical war chariots but rather heavy vehicles with solid wheels, suggesting a migrating population with military capabilities rather than a conventional army (Drews 2000). The presence of women and children in some of these carts reinforces the impression of a people on the move seeking new territory, not merely a raiding force.

Egyptian Military Superiority: The reliefs predictably emphasize Egyptian dominance, showing Ramesses III and his forces slaughtering the Sea Peoples. Egyptian chariotry and infantry are depicted in ordered formations, while the pharaoh himself towers over the battlefield, single-handedly dispatching enemies. Egyptian archers create a hail of arrows that decimates Sea Peoples formations before they can close to melee range.

The accompanying text proclaims:

"Their confederation was the Peleset, Tjeker, Shekelesh, Denyen, and Weshesh, lands united. They laid their hands upon the lands as far as the circuit of the earth, their hearts confident and trusting: 'Our plans will succeed!'" (Kitchen 1996: 18).

This passage explicitly names the five primary groups comprising the Sea Peoples coalition that confronted Egypt, providing crucial evidence for understanding the composition of these forces (Adams and Cohen 2013). The text continues with Ramesses III's response:

"I organized my frontier in Djahi, prepared before them: princes, commanders of garrisons, and maryanu [elite warriors]. I caused the Nile mouth to be prepared like a strong wall with warships, galleys, and coasters, equipped completely... They were manned completely from bow to stern with valiant warriors bearing their arms, soldiers of all the choicest of Egypt, being like lions roaring upon the mountain-tops" (Breasted 1906, Vol. 4: 64).

This description reveals the Egyptian defensive strategy: establishing forward positions in the Levantine region (Djahi) while creating a naval blockade at the Nile Delta to prevent the Sea Peoples from penetrating Egypt's heartland. The reference to "maryanu" is particularly interesting, as this term originally designated chariot warriors of Hurrian origin, suggesting that Egypt's military included foreign professionals or adopted foreign military terminology.

The Captive Parade: Aftermath and Assimilation

A final significant section of the Medinet Habu reliefs shows the aftermath of the conflict: lines of captured Sea Peoples being presented to the gods by Ramesses III (Emanuel 2013). These scenes provide some of our clearest depictions of the different Sea Peoples groups, as they are shown in formal, static poses rather than the dynamic confusion of battle.

The captives are organized by ethnic group, with distinctive physical features and clothing that helped scholars identify different Sea Peoples factions. Accompanying inscriptions label some of these groups, though damage to the reliefs has obscured some identifications. The captives are shown bound, often with distinctive arm positions that Egyptian art used to denote foreign prisoners.

The accompanying text describes the fate of these captives:
"I settled them in strongholds, bound in my name. Their military classes were as numerous as hundred-thousands. I assigned portions for them all with clothing and provisions from the treasuries and granaries every year" (Kitchen 1996: 22).

This passage reveals a crucial aspect of Egyptian policy: rather than simply eliminating the defeated enemies, Ramesses III incorporated many Sea Peoples warriors into the Egyptian military system as mercenary units. This practice, already established with earlier groups like the Sherden, reflected pragmatic Egyptian statecraft that converted former enemies into military assets (Emanuel 2013).

The Composition of the Sea Peoples Coalition

The Medinet Habu inscriptions provide our most explicit enumeration of the Sea Peoples groups that threatened Egypt during Ramesses III's reign. The text specifically names five primary groups—the Peleset, Tjeker, Shekelesh, Denyen, and Weshesh—as forming a coalition or confederation that attacked Egypt both by land and sea (Killebrew and Lehmann 2013). These groups appear to have distinct identities while operating in concert, suggesting a complex political arrangement rather than a single ethnic entity.

The Peleset: Forerunners of the Philistines

The Peleset receive particular attention in the Medinet Habu reliefs, where they are depicted wearing distinctive headdresses composed of upright reeds or feathers arranged in a crown-like formation. Their equipment typically includes round shields, spears, and straight swords. Most scholars now accept the identification of the Peleset with the biblical Philistines who later established a pentapolis of city-states in southern Canaan (modern Israel/Palestine) (Dothan and Dothan 1992).

Archaeological evidence from sites like Ashkelon, Ashdod, and Ekron reveals a material culture that combines Aegean elements with local Canaanite traditions, supporting the narrative of Sea Peoples settlement in this region following their defeat by Egypt (Killebrew 2005). Distinctive pottery styles, architectural features, and dietary practices (particularly a taboo on pork consumption that differs from both Egyptian and Canaanite norms) suggest a population with origins in the Aegean world who adapted to local conditions while maintaining aspects of their cultural identity.

"The archaeological signature of early Philistine settlements includes locally-made pottery that imitates Mycenaean forms," noted archaeologist Trude Dothan, who pioneered the study of Philistine material culture. "This suggests a population with strong cultural connections to the Aegean world who were reproducing familiar forms with local materials" (Dothan 1982: 219).

The Tjeker: Northern Settlers

The Tjeker (also transliterated as Tjekker or Sikil) appear in the Medinet Habu inscriptions as part of the Sea Peoples coalition. While they receive less attention than the Peleset in the reliefs, other sources provide important context for this group. The 11th century BCE Egyptian tale of Wenamun mentions the Tjeker as controlling the Levantine port city of Dor, suggesting they established a territorial foothold in the northern coastal region of modern Israel (Wente 1990).

Archaeological excavations at Dor have revealed material culture with Cypriot and Aegean affiliations dating to the early Iron Age, potentially corresponding to Tjeker settlement (Gilboa, Sharon, and Boaretto 2008). Their control of this important port would have given them significant influence over maritime trade routes in the post-collapse eastern Mediterranean.

The Shekelesh: Western Connection

The Shekelesh (or Sheklesh) had appeared in Egyptian records since the time of Merneptah, when they participated in a Libyan-led invasion of Egypt. Their reappearance in Ramesses III's inscriptions suggests a long-term pattern of interaction with Egypt and the eastern Mediterranean. Many scholars have proposed a connection between the Shekelesh and Sicily, noting the phonetic similarity to the name Sikels (a people mentioned in classical sources as inhabiting eastern Sicily) (Vagnetti 2000).

If this identification is correct, it would extend the geographical range of Sea Peoples activity well into the central Mediterranean, suggesting networks that spanned from the Aegean to the Italian peninsula. Archaeological evidence from Sicily during this period shows disruption and population movement, potentially corresponding to the historical activities of the Shekelesh.

The Denyen: Aegean Origins

The Denyen (also rendered as Danuna or Danunians) have been associated with the Danaans, a term used by Homer to refer to Greeks in the Iliad. Alternative theories connect them to the region of Adana in Cilicia (southern Turkey), where texts from Ugarit mention a kingdom called Danuna (Singer 1999). Either identification would place their origins in the broader Aegean or eastern Mediterranean sphere.

The Medinet Habu reliefs show the Denyen with distinctive headgear and weapons, though damage to portions of the reliefs has made comprehensive analysis challenging. Their inclusion in the Sea Peoples coalition suggests they controlled significant maritime resources and shared common cause with other displaced or opportunistic groups during the Bronze Age collapse.

The Weshesh: Enigmatic Partners

The Weshesh remain the most enigmatic of the five groups named in the Medinet Habu inscriptions. They are not mentioned in earlier Egyptian texts, and no convincing identification with known archaeological cultures or later historical groups has gained scholarly consensus (Woudhuizen 2006). Various proposals have connected them to regions ranging from Crete to western Anatolia, but evidence remains inconclusive.

Their appearance alongside better-documented groups like the Peleset and Tjeker suggests they controlled sufficient resources to be considered a significant component of the Sea Peoples coalition, but their specific contributions and ultimate fate remain obscure.

Egyptian Military Strategy and Tactical Innovations

The Medinet Habu inscriptions and reliefs reveal sophisticated Egyptian military planning in response to the Sea Peoples threat. Ramesses III implemented a comprehensive strategy that combined forward defense in the Levant with a powerful defensive position at the Nile Delta (Mumford 2014). This multi-layered approach reflected lessons learned from earlier invasions during the reigns of Merneptah and Ramesses II.

Forward Defense in the Levant

The inscriptions state that Ramesses III "organized my frontier in Djahi," referring to Egyptian-controlled territories in the southern Levant. This forward deployment allowed Egyptian forces to monitor Sea Peoples movements and potentially disrupt their advance before they reached Egypt proper. Archaeological evidence from sites like Beth Shean in northern Israel shows continued Egyptian presence during this period, with garrison facilities maintained even as other parts of the Levantine system collapsed (Fischer 2014).

The forward defense strategy would have served multiple purposes:

Early Warning System: Egyptian outposts in the Levant could provide intelligence about Sea Peoples movements, allowing time for reinforcement and preparation.

Resource Denial: By maintaining control of fertile Levantine territories, Egypt prevented the Sea Peoples from acquiring agricultural resources that could sustain a larger invasion force.

Divide and Conquer: Egyptian diplomacy could potentially separate some Sea Peoples groups from the coalition through targeted agreements, weakening the overall threat.

The Delta Defense: Integrated Naval and Land Operations

The most innovative aspect of Ramesses III's strategy was the integrated defense of the Nile Delta, combining naval forces with land-based troops in a coordinated operation. The Medinet Habu inscriptions describe this approach:

"I caused the Nile mouth to be prepared like a strong wall with warships, galleys, and coasters, equipped completely... They were manned completely from bow to stern with valiant warriors bearing their arms, soldiers of all the choicest of Egypt, being like lions roaring upon the mountain-tops" (Kitchen 1996: 19).

This description suggests several tactical elements:

Naval Blockade: Egyptian ships were positioned at the Nile mouths to prevent enemy vessels from entering the river system that served as Egypt's primary transportation network.

Amphibious Forces: Egyptian vessels carried both sailors and soldiers, allowing them to engage in ship-to-ship combat or land troops as needed.

Choke Point Exploitation: By forcing the Sea Peoples fleet to engage at the narrow Nile mouths rather than the open sea, Egyptian commanders negated potential enemy advantages in ship maneuverability or numbers.

The relief images support this interpretation, showing Egyptian ships forming what appears to be a defensive line while archers on both vessels and the shoreline concentrate fire on the approaching Sea Peoples ships. The naval tactics depicted represent a significant evolution in maritime warfare, showing coordinated fleet actions rather than the individual ship-to-ship engagements typical of earlier naval combat.

Technological and Tactical Advantages

The Medinet Habu reliefs highlight several Egyptian military advantages that contributed to their victory:

Superior Ranged Weapons: Egyptian archers are prominently featured in both the land and sea battle scenes, creating a crucial advantage through massed missile fire. The Sea Peoples forces appear to rely primarily on close-combat weapons, making them vulnerable during the approach to Egyptian positions.

Integrated Forces: The Egyptian military combined chariotry, infantry, and naval forces in coordinated operations. The reliefs show these different military arms supporting each other, with archers providing covering fire for advancing infantry and chariots delivering mobile strike capability.

Logistical Preparation: Inscriptions emphasize Ramesses III's careful preparation, including stockpiling weapons and positioning forces strategically. This suggests the Egyptian response was not improvised but reflected sophisticated military planning.

Defensive Terrain Exploitation: By choosing to make their stand at the Nile Delta, Egyptian forces utilized familiar terrain that maximized their advantages while creating natural obstacles for the invaders.

The Outcome: Victory and Assimilation

According to the Medinet Habu inscriptions, Ramesses III's strategy resulted in a decisive victory over the Sea Peoples coalition. The reliefs show Egyptian forces triumphant in both the land and sea battles, with enemy warriors killed, captured, or driven back. The accompanying text proclaims:

"Those who reached my frontier, their seed is not, their heart and their soul are finished forever and ever. Those who came forward together on the sea, the full flame was in front of them at the river-mouths, while a stockade of lances surrounded them on the shore. They were dragged in, enclosed, and prostrated on the beach, killed, and made into heaps from tail to head" (Kitchen 1996: 16).

This graphic description emphasizes complete Egyptian victory, though we must approach such claims with appropriate skepticism given the propagandistic nature of royal inscriptions. Nevertheless, archaeological evidence supports the general outline of Egyptian success: Egypt maintained its territorial integrity and political system when many other Bronze Age states collapsed entirely (Cline 2014).

However, the aftermath of the conflict reveals a more complex outcome than simple victory or defeat. The Medinet Habu inscriptions themselves indicate that many captured Sea Peoples warriors were incorporated into the Egyptian military system:

"I settled them in strongholds, bound in my name. Their military classes were as numerous as hundred-thousands. I assigned portions for them all with clothing and provisions from the treasuries and granaries every year" (Kitchen 1996: 22).

This policy of assimilating defeated enemies as military auxiliaries had precedent in Egyptian practice, particularly with the Sherden who had been integrated into Egyptian forces since the reign of Ramesses II (Emanuel 2013). The Sea Peoples groups defeated by Ramesses III thus contributed to Egyptian military power even as they were prevented from conquering Egyptian territory.

Beyond Egypt's borders, archaeological evidence indicates that some Sea Peoples groups—particularly the Peleset and Tjeker—established permanent settlements in the Levantine coastal regions following their defeat (Finkelstein 2000). These settlements would evolve into the Philistine pentapolis and other political entities that played significant roles in the early Iron Age Levant. Rather than returning to their places of origin or dispersing entirely, these groups adapted to new circumstances, creating hybrid cultures that combined elements from their backgrounds with local Canaanite traditions (Yasur-Landau 2010).

Beyond Propaganda: Reading Between the Lines

While the Medinet Habu inscriptions and reliefs present the Sea Peoples conflict as a straightforward Egyptian victory, careful analysis reveals nuances that suggest a more complex historical reality (Ben-Dor Evian 2017). Several aspects of the record invite critical interpretation:

The Defensive Posture: Despite the triumphalist language, the Egyptian strategy as described was fundamentally defensive—focused on protecting the Nile Delta rather than projecting power outward. This suggests Egypt lacked the resources or confidence to engage the Sea Peoples farther from its borders, perhaps indicating a weakened state following earlier conflicts and systemic pressures.

Territorial Concessions: The establishment of Philistine and other Sea Peoples settlements in the Levant—some in territories previously under Egyptian control—suggests that while Egypt protected its core territories, it effectively ceded influence in parts of its former empire (Stern 2000). The concentration of Philistine settlements in southern Canaan may represent a negotiated outcome rather than simply the result of military defeat.

Economic Integration: The incorporation of Sea Peoples warriors into Egyptian military units indicates that Egypt faced manpower shortages that necessitated the recruitment of former enemies. This suggests economic and demographic challenges consistent with the broader Bronze Age system collapse.

"Reading between the lines of the Medinet Habu inscriptions," observed archaeologist Eric Cline, "we can discern a Egypt that successfully weathered the Bronze Age collapse but emerged significantly transformed—more focused on defending its core territories than maintaining the expansive imperial system of the Ramesside period at its height" (Cline 2014: 162).

Conclusion: Pivotal Moment in Mediterranean History

The confrontation between Ramesses III and the Sea Peoples coalition as documented at Medinet Habu represents a pivotal moment in Mediterranean history—the last major battle of the Bronze Age and a crucial transition point toward the emerging Iron Age world (Middleton 2017). The Egyptian victory prevented complete systemic collapse in the eastern Mediterranean, preserving crucial cultural, technological, and institutional knowledge that might otherwise have been lost.

At the same time, the conflict accelerated processes of cultural hybridization and political reconfiguration. The settlement of Sea Peoples groups in the Levant created new political entities with mixed cultural traditions, while Egypt itself began a long process of contraction and transformation (Knapp and Manning 2016). The elaborate military spectacle depicted at Medinet Habu represents both the last triumph of a traditional Bronze Age superpower and the beginning of a new Mediterranean world characterized by more diverse, smaller-scale political entities.

The Sea Peoples were neither simply destroyers of civilization nor innocent refugees, but active participants in a complex process of systemic transformation (Sherratt 2003). Their conflict with Egypt, immortalized in the Medinet Habu reliefs, demonstrates how human agency interacted with broader environmental, economic, and political forces to reshape the Mediterranean world at a crucial historical juncture. In the aftermath of this conflict, new cultural syntheses and political arrangements would emerge that would define the early Iron Age Mediterranean for centuries to come.

Chapter 4

BEYOND EGYPT: THE WIDER DESTRUCTION

Archaeological Evidence Across the Eastern Mediterranean

The year 1200 BCE marked the beginning of a cascade of catastrophes that would fundamentally transform the Eastern Mediterranean world (Cline 2014). While Egyptian records provide our most detailed textual accounts of the Sea Peoples, the true scale of the Bronze Age collapse becomes apparent only when we examine the archaeological record across multiple regions. The destruction was not limited to coastal raids or isolated conflicts, but represented a systemic failure of the interconnected Late Bronze Age world (Knapp and Manning 2016).

The Fall of the Hittite Empire: Multiple Vectors of Collapse

The Hittite Empire, which had dominated Anatolia and contested with Egypt for control of the Levant, disappeared with remarkable suddenness around 1180-1170 BCE (Bryce 2005). For decades, scholars debated whether the Sea Peoples played a direct role in its collapse. The evidence suggests a more complex scenario involving multiple factors, with maritime raiders representing just one component of a perfect storm.

Suppiluliuma II's Final Stand

The last documented Hittite king, Suppiluliuma II (c. 1207-1170 BCE), left records that paint a picture of an empire under severe stress. Tablets from Hattusa describe increasingly desperate measures to secure grain shipments from Egypt, suggesting serious food shortages (Hoffner 2009). One fragmentary letter states: "The situation is severe. The granaries are depleted, and the people cry out for bread."

Particularly revealing is a tablet describing naval battles against seaborne invaders off the coast of Cyprus:

"The ships of the enemy came; they destroyed my cities along the seashore, but I stood against them in the sea, and defeated them there. I seized their ships and set fire to them in the midst of the sea" (Singer 2000: 24).

This text, likely referring to a campaign against either Lukka pirates or early Sea Peoples groups, demonstrates that maritime threats had reached Hittite territory well before the empire's final collapse. The campaign may have temporarily secured Hittite interests in Cyprus, but represented a significant drain on already stretched imperial resources (Karageorghis 1992).

Archaeological Evidence at Hattusa

The archaeological record at Hattusa, the Hittite capital, reveals a planned abandonment rather than violent destruction. Trevor Bryce, a leading Hittite scholar, notes: "The royal archives were selectively culled, with certain tablets deliberately removed while others were left behind. This suggests an organized withdrawal rather than a chaotic flight" (Bryce 2005: 348).

Key religious objects and royal insignia are conspicuously absent from the archaeological record, indicating they were removed before the city's abandonment (Güterbock 1992). The evidence points to a strategic decision to relocate the center of power, possibly in response to multiple threats.

While direct Sea Peoples involvement at Hattusa appears unlikely, coastal Hittite sites tell a different story. Excavations at Mersin and Tarsus on the Mediterranean coast reveal violent destruction layers dating to approximately 1190-1180 BCE (Ward and Joukowsky 1992). At both sites, distinctive pottery with affinities to Aegean styles appears immediately above the destruction layers, suggesting new populations moved in following the cities' fall.

Climate Change and the Hittite Collapse

Paleoclimatic data provides crucial context for understanding the Hittite collapse. Oxygen isotope analysis from Nar Gölü, a crater lake in central Anatolia, indicates a significant shift toward drier conditions beginning around 1200 BCE (Kaniewski et al. 2010). This climate change would have severely impacted agricultural production in the Hittite heartland, which relied heavily on rainfall agriculture.

The Hittite kingdom was particularly vulnerable to climate disruption due to its geographic position. As archaeologist Neil Roberts explains: "Central Anatolia sits at a climatic crossroads, where relatively minor shifts in atmospheric circulation patterns can have dramatic effects on precipitation. The Hittite agricultural system had developed during an unusually stable and favorable climatic period that ended abruptly around 1200 BCE" (Manning 2013: 482).

Pollen cores from across Anatolia show a marked decline in cultivated cereal pollens and an increase in drought-resistant species during this period, confirming agricultural disruption. This environmental stress likely triggered population movements, including some groups who would later be identified among the Sea Peoples.

A Systemic Collapse

The Hittite collapse thus appears to represent a classic case of systemic failure, where multiple stress factors—climate change, food insecurity, population movements, and military threats—created a cascade of problems that overwhelmed the state's capacity to respond (Middleton 2017). The Sea Peoples were not the sole cause of the Hittite collapse, but rather one manifestation of broader regional instability.

As Hittitologist Itamar Singer concluded: "The Hittite Empire did not fall solely to external invasion, but collapsed under the weight of internal weaknesses exacerbated by climate change, economic disruption, and population movements. Some groups later identified among the 'Sea Peoples' may have delivered the coup de grâce to an already failing system, particularly in coastal regions, but they were symptoms of collapse as much as its cause" (Singer 2000: 31).

The Mycenaean Catastrophe: Greece in Flames

The collapse of Mycenaean civilization in Greece provides another critical perspective on the Bronze Age collapse (Dickinson 2006). Between approximately 1250 and 1190 BCE, virtually every major Mycenaean palace center was destroyed, including Mycenae, Tiryns, Pylos, Thebes, and Orchomenos. This catastrophe fundamentally transformed Greek society, leading to population decline, technological regression, and cultural discontinuity.

The Archaeological Evidence

The destruction of the Mycenaean palaces is vividly preserved in the archaeological record. At Pylos, excavations revealed the Palace of Nestor consumed by a fire so intense that clay tablets were accidentally fired and preserved, providing a snapshot of the final days before destruction (Davis 2008). These Linear B administrative records show no awareness of imminent threat, suggesting the attack came with little warning.

At Mycenae itself, the archaeological evidence indicates multiple destruction events. The first occurred around 1250 BCE, after which the city's famous Cyclopean walls were extended and water supply systems improved—clear evidence of increasing concern about security (Burke 2008). A final destruction around 1190 BCE effectively ended Mycenae's role as a palace center.

Particularly telling is the evidence from smaller settlements. Archaeologist James Wright observes: "It wasn't just the major centers that were destroyed. We see a pattern of abandonment and destruction across settlements of all sizes, suggesting widespread instability rather than targeted attacks on centers of power" (Maran 2009: 253).

Internal Conflict or External Invasion?

The question of who destroyed the Mycenaean palaces has generated intense scholarly debate. Earlier theories emphasized invasion, potentially connecting the destruction to Sea Peoples or "Dorian" invasions from the north. More recent scholarship has increasingly emphasized internal factors (Middleton 2010).

The archaeological evidence presents a mixed picture. Some sites show clear signs of violent conflict, including unburied bodies and weaponry found in destruction layers. At Tiryns, for example, arrowheads embedded in walls suggest intense fighting. Other sites, however, show evidence of fire but no clear indicators of warfare.

The pattern of destruction is also telling. As archaeologist Eric Cline notes: "The destructions weren't simultaneous but occurred over a period of decades, with some sites destroyed and rebuilt multiple times. This pattern is more consistent with ongoing instability than a single invasion event" (Cline 2014: 98).

The Linear B tablets provide indirect evidence for internal stress before the final collapse. Records from Pylos mention coastal watchers and the redeployment of bronze from sanctuaries to produce weapons, suggesting concern about maritime raids (Kelder 2010). Other tablets record the special provision of offerings to deities, possibly indicating religious responses to perceived crises.

Mycenaeans Among the Sea Peoples?

An intriguing possibility is that some Mycenaean Greeks themselves became part of the Sea Peoples phenomenon following the destruction of their home communities. The Ekwesh mentioned in Egyptian records have been tentatively identified with the Ahhiyawa (Achaeans) known from Hittite texts (Beckman, Bryce, and Cline 2011). Similarly, the Denyen might correspond to the Danaans, another term for Greeks in Homer.

Material evidence potentially supporting this connection comes from Philistine settlements in the Levant, where early Iron Age pottery shows clear Mycenaean influence. As archaeologist Assaf Yasur-Landau argues: "The material culture of the early Philistines suggests that at least some of their population originated in the Aegean world, bringing with them cultural practices that were adapted to their new environment" (Yasur-Landau 2010: 167).

This scenario suggests that the collapse of Mycenaean palace society may have released population groups who, facing limited prospects at home, joined the broader movement of peoples around the Mediterranean—some eventually becoming part of the Sea Peoples phenomenon that Egyptian sources describe.

Systemic Collapse in the Aegean

The Mycenaean collapse, like the Hittite one, is best understood as a systemic failure triggered by multiple interacting factors. Climate change affected agricultural productivity, potentially creating food insecurity. The highly centralized palace economy, documented in Linear B tablets, lacked resilience when faced with environmental stress and potential conflict.

The archaeological evidence for improved fortifications and emergency water supplies at multiple sites indicates that Mycenaean elites perceived growing threats but proved unable to maintain the complex palace system in the face of multiple challenges. Whether the final blows came from external invaders, internal uprisings, or some combination of factors, the result was a fundamental transformation of Aegean society.

Ugarit: A City's Final Hours

Perhaps no site provides more vivid evidence of the Bronze Age collapse than the coastal Syrian city of Ugarit (Yon 1992). A thriving international port and administrative center, Ugarit was destroyed suddenly around 1185 BCE, with its ruins remaining undiscovered until 1928. The excavations revealed a wealthy city destroyed at the height of its prosperity, with archives of clay tablets preserved by the fire that consumed the city.

The Last Days of Ugarit

The tablets discovered at Ugarit include correspondence that provides a rare glimpse into the final days of a Bronze Age city. A letter from the last king of Ugarit, Ammurapi, to the king of Alashiya (Cyprus) conveys the desperate situation:

"My father, behold, the enemy ships are coming. They have set fire to my cities and have done very great damage in the country. Does my father not know that all my troops are stationed in Hittite country, and all my ships are stationed in

Lycia? They have not yet returned, so the country is abandoned to itself. May my father know it: seven enemy ships have come and done very great damage" (Pardee 2003: 101).

Another tablet, found in the oven where it was apparently being prepared for firing when the attack came, contains a message from a military officer named Eshuwara reporting that the situation was under control—a tragic testament to how quickly the city fell (Schaeffer 1968).

Archaeological evidence confirms the textual accounts of a sudden, violent end. Human remains found in the destruction layer suggest some inhabitants were killed during the attack (Ussishkin 1985). The city's substantial fortifications proved inadequate against the assault, and unlike some other destroyed centers, Ugarit was never reoccupied as a major urban center.

The Perpetrators Question

While the Ugarit texts clearly describe an attack by sea, they don't identify the attackers by name. Were they Sea Peoples groups known from Egyptian records, or other maritime raiders? The timing correlates closely with Ramesses III's accounts of Sea Peoples activity, suggesting a possible connection.

Material evidence from the destruction layer provides some clues. Archaeologist Marguerite Yon notes: "Arrowheads of unfamiliar types were found embedded in walls and scattered throughout destruction contexts, suggesting attackers using weapons not typical of Ugarit's defenders" (Yon 1992: 119).

Some scholars have proposed that ships described in the Medinet Habu reliefs as belonging to the Sea Peoples—with distinctive bird-head prows—may represent the same vessels that attacked Ugarit. However, no definitive evidence links specific Sea Peoples groups to Ugarit's destruction.

Economic Implications

Ugarit's destruction had significant ripple effects throughout the Eastern Mediterranean economic system. The city had served as a crucial node in regional trade networks, connecting Mesopotamia, Egypt, Anatolia, and the Aegean (Routledge and McGeough 2009). Cuneiform tablets document Ugarit's role in the tin trade, essential for bronze production throughout the region.

One tablet records a shipment of "ten talents of fine copper and 8,000 shekels of tin" destined for workshops in the Aegean—a shipment that likely never arrived. The disruption of such trade routes would have had cascading effects on bronze production throughout the region, potentially contributing to the transition to iron technology that characterizes the subsequent period.

Troy: Myth and Archaeological Reality

The site of Troy (Hisarlik in modern Turkey) occupies a special place in discussions of the Bronze Age collapse, due both to its strategic location at the entrance to the Dardanelles and its connection to Homeric epic (Cline 2009). The archaeological level traditionally identified as "Homer's Troy" (Troy VIIa) was indeed destroyed around 1180 BCE, during the broader Bronze Age collapse.

The Evidence from Troy VIIa

Excavations at Troy reveal that Troy VIIa met a violent end. Archaeologist Manfred Korfmann described the evidence: "We find arrowheads embedded in walls and streets, unburied human remains, and valuable objects abandoned in buildings—all indicating a sudden attack rather than planned abandonment" (Korfmann cited in Cline 2009: 362).

The destruction layer contains evidence of intense fire, with mud-brick walls baked hard by the heat. Following this destruction, the site was reoccupied (Troy VIIb), but with significant changes in material culture, including the appearance of handmade "knobbed ware" pottery associated with Balkan populations—suggesting new groups moved into the area after Troy's fall.

Troy and the Sea Peoples Connection

Was Troy destroyed by groups associated with the Sea Peoples? The archaeological evidence neither confirms nor refutes this possibility. The site's destruction falls within the timeframe of Sea Peoples activity known from Egyptian sources, but no inscriptions or distinctive Sea Peoples artifacts have been found at Troy.

An intriguing possibility is that Troy's destruction relates to broader population movements from the Balkans. Some scholars have suggested that certain Sea Peoples groups, particularly the Shekelesh and Teresh, may have originated in Thrace or other Balkan regions (Jung 2018). These movements might have affected Troy as populations shifted southward toward the Mediterranean.

The discovery of Mycenaean-style pottery and weapons at Troy VI and VIIa demonstrates the site's connection to Aegean trade networks (Mountjoy 1998). The disruption of these networks during the Bronze Age collapse would have severely impacted Troy's economy, potentially making it vulnerable to attack or internal instability.

The Economic Dimensions of Collapse

The Bronze Age Mediterranean functioned as an integrated economic system, with specialized production centers connected by maritime and overland trade routes (Sherratt 2003). This system's complexity was both a strength and a vulnerability—creating prosperity during stable periods but susceptible to cascading failures when key nodes were disrupted.

The Metals Trade Disruption

Bronze production required tin, which was scarce in the Mediterranean region and often imported from distant sources. Archaeological and textual evidence suggests tin came from as far as Afghanistan or Britain, traveling along complex trade routes vulnerable to disruption (Pulak 2008).

The destruction of key trading centers like Ugarit and the collapse of palace economies that organized long-distance exchange severely impacted metal supplies. Archaeometallurgist James Muhly observes: "We see evidence for metal hoarding and recycling intensifying during the collapse period, suggesting severe supply constraints" (cited in Sherratt 2003: 52).

This disruption likely accelerated the transition to iron technology that characterizes the early Iron Age. While iron was more abundant than tin, it required different production techniques. The knowledge for ironworking may have been preserved and transmitted by specialized metalworking groups, some possibly associated with Sea Peoples populations.

Agricultural Systems Under Stress

Paleoclimatic data indicates that the period around 1200 BCE experienced significant climate deterioration across the Eastern Mediterranean (Kaniewski et al. 2013). Tree ring studies from Anatolia show reduced growth patterns, while pollen cores from Greece, Anatolia, and the Levant indicate declining agricultural productivity.

The highly centralized palace economies of the Late Bronze Age were especially vulnerable to agricultural disruption. These systems relied on specialized production and redistribution, with limited flexibility to adapt to changing conditions. When climate stress reduced agricultural output, the elaborate bureaucratic structures became unsustainable.

At Pylos, Linear B tablets record the palace's tight control over agricultural production and food distribution. When this system collapsed, local communities would have needed to reorganize subsistence strategies with fewer resources and reduced coordination capacity, potentially leading to significant population decline.

Beyond Collapse: Seeds of Transformation

While the Bronze Age collapse represented a significant civilizational regression in many respects—with population decline, reduced literacy, and technological simplification—it also created conditions for innovation and new social formations (Wengrow 2010). The Sea Peoples, often portrayed simply as destroyers, played a more complex role in this transformation.

The Philistine Case Study

The clearest example of Sea Peoples as agents of cultural transformation comes from the Philistines, who established a distinctive culture in the southern Levant following the collapse (Maeir and Hitchcock 2017). Archaeological excavations at sites like Ashkelon, Ashdod, and Ekron reveal a hybrid culture combining Aegean, Cypriot, and Levantine elements.

Archaeologist Ann Killebrew describes this process: "Rather than simple replacement or acculturation, we see a complex negotiation of identity, with certain Aegean cultural practices maintained and adapted to local conditions while others were abandoned. This suggests the integration of multiple population elements rather than a simple invasion scenario" (Killebrew 2005: 197).

The Philistines developed distinctive cultural practices, including unique pottery styles, dietary preferences (evidenced by the consumption of pork, rare in other Levantine contexts), architectural elements, and eventually their own script (Stager 1995). Their political organization into a pentapolis (five main cities) represented an innovative adaptation to post-collapse conditions.

New Trade Networks and Iron Technology

As the old palace-centered trade systems collapsed, new, more decentralized networks emerged. Phoenician city-states like Tyre, Sidon, and Byblos—which survived the collapse with less disruption than many regions—became crucial nodes in these new networks, eventually expanding trade connections westward across the Mediterranean (Bell 2006).

The transition to iron technology accelerated in the post-collapse period. While iron was known in the Late Bronze Age, it became the dominant metal for tools and weapons only after the collapse disrupted bronze production networks. This technological shift had profound social implications, potentially democratizing access to metal tools that had previously been more tightly controlled by elites.

Reassessing the Sea Peoples Phenomenon

The archaeological evidence across the Eastern Mediterranean suggests that the Sea Peoples were not simply external invaders who destroyed Bronze Age civilizations, but part of a complex process of systems collapse and reorganization (Fischer 2007). They appear to have included diverse groups—some displaced by climate change and political instability, others opportunistically taking advantage of weakened states, and still others representing local populations adapting to changing circumstances.

From Raiders to Settlers

The trajectory from maritime raiding to settlement is documented not only for the Philistines but also for other groups. In northern Syria, distinctive pottery assemblages at sites like Tell Tayinat suggest the presence of Aegean-influenced populations following the collapse, possibly corresponding to the Denyen mentioned in Egyptian texts (Janeway 2006-2007).

This pattern—maritime raiding followed by settlement—has historical parallels in later Mediterranean history, including the Viking expansions of the early medieval period. It represents a strategic adaptation to changing opportunities, rather than a predetermined plan of conquest.

Agency and Victimhood

The Sea Peoples thus occupied a complex position as both agents and victims of the Bronze Age collapse. Some groups were likely displaced by the same processes of climate change and political instability that they subsequently exacerbated through their movements and actions. Others may have been opportunistic predators taking advantage of weakened states.

This nuanced understanding helps explain the archaeological patterns we observe—not a simple story of invaders destroying civilizations, but a complex process of system failure involving multiple interacting factors, with human groups adapting and responding to changing conditions in diverse ways (Molloy 2016).

Conclusion: Collapse as Process

The archaeological evidence from Hittite Anatolia, Mycenaean Greece, Ugarit, Troy, and other sites reveals the Bronze Age collapse as a complex, multifaceted process rather than a single event (Monroe 2009). The Sea Peoples played an important role in this process, but they operated within a broader context of climate change, political instability, and economic disruption.

What makes the Bronze Age collapse so significant is not simply that individual cities or states failed—this had happened throughout history—but that an entire international system disintegrated. The interconnected, specialized world of the Late Bronze Age gave way to a more fragmented, localized early Iron Age landscape (Van De Mieroop 2016).

Yet within this collapse lay the seeds of regeneration. New political formations, technologies, and cultural syntheses emerged from the ashes of the Bronze Age world. The Sea Peoples, particularly groups like the Philistines, contributed to these innovations, creating hybrid cultures that would influence subsequent Mediterranean history.

The Bronze Age collapse thus serves as a powerful case study in how complex societies respond to multiple, interacting stressors. When climate change, population movements, economic disruption, and political instability converged around 1200 BCE, even sophisticated civilizations with centuries of history proved vulnerable. Understanding this process provides valuable perspective on system resilience and failure that remains relevant to modern concerns about climate change and societal sustainability (Nur and Cline 2000).

As we piece together the archaeological evidence from destruction layers across the Eastern Mediterranean, we gain not just knowledge about a past catastrophe, but insights into how human societies adapt, transform, and rebuild in the face of existential challenges.

Chapter 5

R JAY DRISKILL

THE MECHANICS OF COLLAPSE

The Art of Destruction: Sea Peoples' Military Capabilities

The archaeological and textual evidence regarding the Sea Peoples' military tactics presents us with a complex picture that defies simplistic characterization. While Egyptian sources naturally emphasize their own victories, a careful analysis of both iconographic and archaeological evidence reveals sophisticated capabilities that contributed to these groups' impact across the Mediterranean.

Naval Warfare: Masters of Maritime Mobility

The most distinctive aspect of Sea Peoples warfare was their naval capability. The reliefs at Medinet Habu provide our most detailed visual representation of their vessels, depicting ships with high, curved stems and sterns, often adorned with bird-head prows (Roberts 2009). These vessels differ markedly from Egyptian ships shown in the same reliefs, which feature lower profiles and papyriform decorations.

"The naval battle scenes at Medinet Habu represent a watershed moment in ancient Mediterranean military history," notes naval historian John Hale. "They are the first detailed depiction of a sea battle in ancient art, and they show two distinctly different naval traditions clashing" (cited in Wachsmann 1998: 203).

Analysis of these representations suggests the Sea Peoples employed vessels optimized for different purposes than Egyptian ships. While Egyptian vessels were designed primarily for riverine transport and coastal operations, the Sea Peoples' ships appear better suited to open-water navigation. Their higher freeboard (the distance from the waterline to the upper deck) would have provided better performance in rough seas, while their apparently shallower draft would have allowed beaching operations on a wider range of coastlines (Bass 1967).

The tactical implications were significant. Sea Peoples groups could project power rapidly along coastlines, appearing with little warning and withdrawing before substantial defensive forces could be mustered. A letter found at Ugarit vividly illustrates this threat:

"The enemy ships are coming, and they are burning my cities with fire. They are doing unseemly things in the land... My father, behold, the enemy's ships came; my cities were burned, and they did evil things in my land" (Pardee 2003: 101).

This mobility advantage was partially neutralized in the Nile Delta campaign depicted at Medinet Habu, where Ramesses III implemented a sophisticated defensive strategy. The Egyptian reliefs show their forces deploying a combination of ship-based archers and a blocking line of vessels to trap the Sea Peoples in a naval ambush. The accompanying text boasts:

"Those who reached my boundary, their seed is not; their heart and their soul are finished forever and ever. As for those who had assembled before them on the sea, the full flame was in their front before the harbor-mouths, and a wall of metal upon the shore surrounded them" (Kitchen 1996: 16).

Archaeological evidence from shipwrecks like Point Iria and Cape Gelidonya, dating to this period, provides additional insights into seafaring technology of the era (Bass 1967; Pulak 1998). While we cannot definitively attribute these wrecks to Sea Peoples vessels, they demonstrate the capabilities of Late Bronze Age ships to carry substantial cargoes—capabilities that could be repurposed for troop transport and raiding operations.

The naval expertise displayed by Sea Peoples groups suggests long experience with maritime activities, supporting theories that connect at least some of these populations to coastal regions of the Aegean, western Anatolia, or the central

Mediterranean (Artzy 1997). Their ability to coordinate substantial fleets further indicates organizational capabilities beyond simple piracy, pointing to more complex social structures capable of mounting sustained campaigns.

Land Warfare: Tactical Innovations

While their naval capabilities enabled strategic mobility, the Sea Peoples' land forces executed the actual destruction documented at numerous archaeological sites. The Medinet Habu reliefs provide our most detailed visual evidence of their land warfare capabilities, showing distinctive warriors with various types of equipment (Ben-Dor Evian 2016).

Several tactical advantages appear to have contributed to their battlefield effectiveness:

1. Combined Arms Approach

The reliefs show Sea Peoples forces employing a combination of infantry types, including heavily-armed close-combat troops with swords and spears, alongside lighter infantry with javelins. They are also depicted with ox-drawn carts carrying women and children, suggesting operations as complete population movements rather than merely military expeditions (Drews 2000).

"What we see is not simply a raiding force," argues military historian Robert Drews, "but a complete society on the move, with warriors protecting non-combatants in a migration under arms" (Drews 1993: 48).

This mixed composition offered tactical flexibility, allowing Sea Peoples forces to adapt to different battlefield conditions. The presence of families also suggests high motivation—these were not merely mercenaries, but people fighting for new homelands.

2. Distinctive Weaponry and Armor

The Medinet Habu reliefs show Sea Peoples warriors with equipment that differs significantly from Egyptian and Near Eastern norms (Sandars 1985). Many are depicted wearing distinctive feathered or horned headdresses and using what appear to be bronze or iron swords of various designs.

Some groups, particularly the Sherden, are shown with distinctive round shields and horned helmets, while others like the Peleset appear with feathered headdresses and smaller round shields. This equipment suggests specialized warrior traditions with their own tactical doctrines, rather than ad hoc raiding bands.

Archaeological discoveries provide physical evidence of these weapon systems. At Bademgediği Tepe in western Anatolia, excavations revealed a destruction layer dating to around 1200 BCE containing Naue II type swords—a cutting and thrusting weapon that represented an innovation over the primarily thrusting swords common in earlier periods (Jung 2009). Similar weapons have been found at sites across the Mediterranean in contexts associated with the collapse period.

3. Psychological Warfare

Several scholars have suggested that the distinctive appearance of Sea Peoples warriors—with their feathered headdresses, horned helmets, and foreign equipment—may have served a psychological warfare function, intimidating opponents (Hitchcock and Maeir 2016). The emphasis on these visual elements in Egyptian depictions suggests they made a strong impression on contemporary observers.

The pattern of destruction visible in the archaeological record—with sites from Greece to the Levant showing evidence of burning and abandonment in a relatively short timeframe—may reflect not just military effectiveness but also the psychological impact of these attacks, potentially triggering preemptive abandonment of some settlements (Zuckerman 2007).

Iron and Bronze: The Metallurgical Question

One of the most persistent questions regarding the Sea Peoples concerns their potential use of iron weapons as a military advantage. The chronology is suggestive—the Bronze Age collapse coincides with the early transition to iron technology in the Mediterranean, and the subsequent Iron Age sees the widespread adoption of iron weaponry. However, the evidence requires careful examination.

The State of Iron Technology circa 1200 BCE

Iron was not unknown in the Late Bronze Age. Prestigious iron objects appear in elite contexts well before the collapse, including an iron dagger in Tutankhamun's tomb (14th century BCE) and iron artifacts at various Mycenaean sites (Muhly 1985). However, these represent relatively rare, high-status items rather than common military equipment.

The technological limitation was not knowledge of iron itself, but mastery of carburization and quenching techniques that transform relatively soft wrought iron into harder steel. The evidence suggests these techniques were still developing during the collapse period.

"The early iron weapons were not necessarily superior to high-quality bronze," notes archaeometallurgist James Muhly. "The advantage of iron lay not in its immediate military applications, but in its greater geological availability compared to tin, an essential component of bronze that required long-distance trade networks" (cited in Sherratt 2003: 51).

Archaeological evidence from the period shows a mixed picture:

The chronological evidence thus suggests that while iron technology was emerging during the collapse period, it had not yet developed to the point where it would provide a decisive military advantage. The disruption of tin supply networks caused by the collapse may have accelerated the transition to iron, making it a consequence rather than a cause of the broader system failure.

Bronze Supply Disruption as a Factor

More significant than any iron advantage was likely the disruption to bronze production. Bronze weaponry depended on tin, which was not widely available in the eastern Mediterranean and required long-distance trade networks—possibly extending as far as Afghanistan or Britain (Pulak 2008).

As political instability spread across the region around 1200 BCE, these supply networks became increasingly vulnerable. A letter from Ugarit, shortly before its destruction, hints at these problems:

"There is famine in our house. We will all die of hunger. If there is grain, give us grain. What shall I give to my subjects to eat?" (Singer 1999: 719).

Without reliable access to tin, even advanced bronze-working societies would have faced difficulties maintaining their military equipment. This vulnerability may have created a spiral effect, where initial disruptions led to weakened defenses, leading to further disruptions.

The Sea Peoples, operating as mobile groups less dependent on fixed infrastructure, may have been better positioned to adapt to these changing material conditions. Their ability to salvage and repurpose metal from conquered territories could have provided a short-term advantage over more institutionalized forces dependent on regular supply chains.

Beyond the Battlefield: Systemic Factors in the Collapse

While military confrontations with Sea Peoples groups represent the most dramatic manifestations of the Bronze Age collapse, a comprehensive understanding requires examining broader systemic factors. The archaeological evidence increasingly points to a complex interaction of multiple stressors that created conditions where mobile groups could catalyze a wider system failure (Middleton 2017).

Climate Deterioration: The Environmental Context

Paleoclimatic research has revealed compelling evidence for significant climate change coinciding with the collapse period. Multiple independent proxy records indicate a shift toward drier conditions across the eastern Mediterranean between approximately 1250-1100 BCE (Kaniewski et al. 2013):

A 2013 study published in PLOS ONE by Kaniewski et al. concluded: "The pollen-derived climatic proxy points to a significant increase of drought during the Sea People event, with dry conditions lasting from ca. 1200 to 850 BCE, and especially pronounced between 1200 and 1100 BCE" (Kaniewski et al. 2013: 8).

These environmental stresses would have had cascading effects on agricultural production. The palatial economies of the Late Bronze Age were particularly vulnerable, as they relied on agricultural surplus extraction to maintain specialized craftspeople, administrators, and military forces (Van De Mieroop 2016). Texts from Ugarit and Hatti reference grain shortages and famine conditions in the final decades before their collapse.

Importantly, climate deterioration would have affected different regions with varying severity, potentially creating population pressures and triggering migration from the most affected areas. This pattern aligns with the apparent north-to-south movement of many Sea Peoples groups, from the Aegean and Anatolia toward the relatively more stable Egyptian territories.

Political Fragility: Internal Contradictions

The Late Bronze Age political systems exhibited structural vulnerabilities that climate stress and external pressure could exploit. These palatial states relied on complex administrative hierarchies to extract and redistribute resources, systems that functioned well during periods of stability but proved brittle under stress (Kelder 2010).

Archaeological evidence from Mycenaean Greece reveals increasing fortification of palaces during the 13th century BCE, suggesting growing internal tensions before any external attacks (Burke 2008). Linear B tablets from Pylos reference coastal watchers and unusual troop deployments shortly before the palace's destruction, indicating perceived threats from both within and without.

In the Hittite realm, succession disputes weakened central authority in the decades before collapse. A letter from the last-known Hittite king, Suppiluliuma II, to the king of Ugarit requesting grain suggests diminishing royal capacity to address basic needs:

"The matter of the grain is life or death to us. If there is no grain, then you must send us grain in ships" (Hoffner 2009: 185).

These internal weaknesses created conditions where external shocks—whether climate events, population movements, or military defeats—could trigger rapid system failure rather than adaptation.

Economic Disruption: The Network Effect

Perhaps the most distinctive feature of the Late Bronze Age was its interconnected economy, with specialized production centers linked by maritime and overland trade routes (Sherratt 2003). Archaeological evidence for this system includes shipwrecks like Uluburun, carrying diverse cargoes of copper, tin, glass, ivory, and finished goods between multiple polities (Bass et al. 1989).

This interconnection created efficiency but also vulnerability—disruption in one region could cascade through the system. Evidence for this network effect includes:

As archaeologist Cyprian Broodbank observes: "What collapsed around 1200 BCE was not just individual states, but an entire international system of goods flow, information exchange, and elite culture" (Broodbank 2013: 423).

In this context, Sea Peoples movements may be better understood as both symptom and cause of system failure. Initial disruptions—whether from climate stress, political instability, or localized conflicts—could have triggered population movements that further stressed the system, eventually reaching a tipping point where recovery became impossible.

Systems Collapse Theory: A Unified Framework

The concept of "systems collapse," developed by archaeologist Colin Renfrew and refined by others, provides a useful framework for understanding how these various factors interacted (Middleton 2017). In this model, complex societies maintain themselves through a series of interconnected subsystems—political, economic, ideological, and environmental. When multiple subsystems experience stress simultaneously, the society's adaptive capacity can be overwhelmed.

The archaeological evidence from the Bronze Age collapse aligns remarkably well with this theoretical framework:

The collapse proceeded not as a single event but as a cascading failure across these subsystems. Initial stresses in one area—such as climate-induced agricultural shortfalls—required adaptive responses that stressed other subsystems, such as increased taxation or labor demands, which in turn undermined political legitimacy.

Sea Peoples groups, operating outside the constraints of the palatial systems, could exploit these vulnerabilities. Their maritime mobility allowed them to target weak points in the system, accelerating the collapse process through what military theorists would call a "force multiplier" effect.

Case Studies in Collapse: Archaeological Signatures

The archaeological record provides several well-documented cases that illustrate how these various factors—Sea Peoples attacks, climate stress, internal contradictions, and system disruptions—manifested in specific contexts.

Ugarit: Catastrophic Failure

The destruction of Ugarit (modern Ras Shamra in Syria) around 1185 BCE represents perhaps the most vivid archaeological case study of the collapse (Yon 1992). This wealthy trading city was destroyed suddenly and violently, with tablets left in kilns and valuable objects abandoned in buildings.

The textual evidence is particularly poignant. Letters discovered in the "House of Urtenu" document the final days of the kingdom, with increasingly desperate communications about enemy ships, food shortages, and military threats. One tablet records:

"When your messenger arrived, the army was humiliated and the city was sacked. Our food in the threshing floors was burnt and the vineyards were also destroyed. Our city is sacked. May you know it! May you know it!" (Schaeffer 1968: 87).

The archaeological context of these tablets—found unfired in kilns, apparently abandoned during the emergency—suggests events unfolded too rapidly for effective response. The destruction layer contains evidence of intense burning throughout the city, with collapsed architecture and scattered valuable objects indicating hasty abandonment.

What makes Ugarit particularly significant is that it represents a wealthy trade center rather than a major political capital. Its destruction demonstrates that the collapse affected not just palatial centers but the entire economic network of the eastern Mediterranean.

Mycenaean Greece: Systemic Failure

The collapse of Mycenaean civilization presents a more complex archaeological signature, with destruction occurring at different centers over several decades (ca. 1250-1190 BCE) (Dickinson 2006). Major palaces including Mycenae, Tiryns, Pylos, and Thebes show evidence of fire destruction, though with important variations in timing and intensity.

At Pylos, Linear B tablets document frantic preparations shortly before destruction, including coastal watches and unusual troop deployments. The palace was then destroyed in a catastrophic fire that ironically preserved these clay documents by baking them (Davis 2008).

Other centers show evidence of adaptation before final abandonment. At Tiryns and Mycenae, lower towns were contracted and additional fortifications constructed in apparent response to increasing threats. These defensive measures proved insufficient, as both sites show subsequent destruction layers.

The post-destruction evidence is equally significant—population decline, abandonment of monumental architecture, cessation of long-distance trade, and the disappearance of writing. This pattern suggests not merely military defeat but comprehensive system failure affecting all aspects of Mycenaean society.

Philistine Settlements: Transformation and Adaptation

The establishment of Philistine settlements in the southern Levant after 1175 BCE provides a crucial counterpoint, showing how some Sea Peoples groups transitioned from maritime raiders to settled populations (Yasur-Landau 2010).

Archaeological excavations at sites like Ashkelon, Ashdod, and Ekron reveal distinctive material culture with Aegean connections, including pottery styles, culinary practices (evidenced by pig consumption), architectural elements, and female figurines (Killebrew 2005). This material assemblage suggests population movement rather than merely cultural diffusion.

What makes the Philistine case particularly interesting is the evidence for hybridization over time. The initial settlement phase shows the strongest Aegean connections, while subsequent phases demonstrate increasing integration of local Canaanite elements alongside retained Aegean features (Stager 1995). This pattern suggests a complex process of cultural negotiation rather than simple replacement.

The Philistine case demonstrates that the collapse, while catastrophic for established powers, created opportunities for new social formations. These former "Sea Peoples" established a successful post-collapse adaptation that would influence the subsequent development of the Levant for centuries.

Synthesis: The Sea Peoples in Context

When we integrate the evidence from military tactics, metallurgical technology, climate studies, and systems theory, a more nuanced understanding of the Sea Peoples phenomenon emerges. Rather than viewing them simply as invaders who caused the collapse, we can recognize them as both agents and products of a complex systemic transformation (Fischer 2007).

The Sea Peoples groups appear to have possessed several advantages that allowed them to thrive during this period of instability:

These advantages became particularly significant in the context of climate deterioration, which stressed agricultural systems and triggered resource competition. The palatial economies, with their specialized production and administrative overhead, proved less resilient than more mobile, adaptable groups.

The collapse itself is best understood as a process rather than an event—a cascading failure where initial disruptions triggered responses that further stressed the system. Sea Peoples movements represent one element in this process, both responding to and accelerating broader patterns of transformation.

This perspective helps explain the archaeological pattern of selective destruction. Sites connected to palatial administration and international trade show the most evidence of violent destruction, while smaller, less specialized settlements often show continuity through the collapse period. This pattern aligns with systems collapse theory, where the most complex, specialized components of a system prove most vulnerable to disruption.

Conclusions: Lessons from the Bronze Age Apocalypse

The evidence regarding Sea Peoples warfare capabilities, combined with our understanding of broader systemic factors, offers several important conclusions:

The Bronze Age collapse offers a sobering case study in how seemingly robust civilizations can experience rapid, catastrophic failure when multiple stressors coincide (Cline 2014). The interdependence that created prosperity during stable periods became a vulnerability when the system faced simultaneous challenges across multiple domains.

Yet the aftermath also demonstrates human resilience and adaptability. New political forms emerged from the collapse—including the Phoenician city-states, the Neo-Hittite kingdoms, and eventually the Greek poleis—that would shape the subsequent Iron Age Mediterranean world (Weeden 2013). Former Sea Peoples groups like the Philistines contributed to this cultural regeneration, developing innovative hybrid societies in their settlement regions.

This pattern of collapse and regeneration offers perspective on our own complex global systems. Like the Late Bronze Age world, our interconnected economies create both efficiency and vulnerability. Understanding how past societies navigated system transformation—whether successfully like the Philistines or catastrophically like Ugarit—may provide valuable insights as we face our own environmental, political, and economic challenges in the twenty-first century.

The Sea Peoples remain enigmatic in many respects, but their role in the Bronze Age collapse illustrates a fundamental historical pattern—that periods of crisis create opportunities for groups able to adapt quickly, while threatening institutions invested in maintaining existing structures. As we piece together the archaeological evidence of their activities, we gain not just knowledge about ancient warfare and collapse, but insight into processes of historical transformation that continue to shape human societies.

Chapter 6

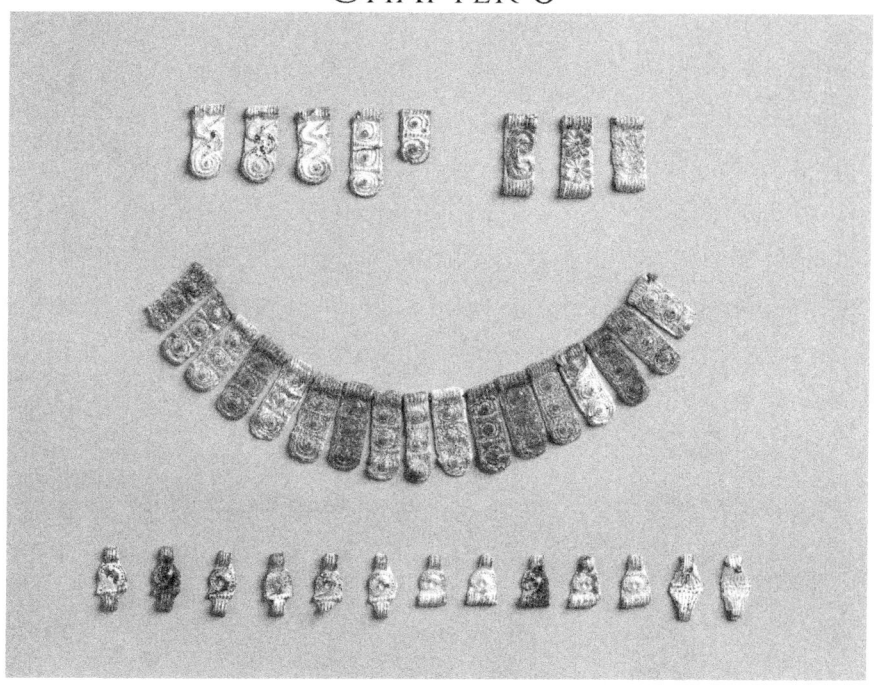

Settling In: The Philistines and Others

The Post-Collapse Mediterranean

The transformation of the eastern Mediterranean after the Bronze Age collapse was neither uniform nor instantaneous. As the dust settled over abandoned palaces and burned citadels around 1150-1100 BCE, survivors began the long process of adaptation and rebuilding (Knapp and Manning 2016). The international system that had connected Egypt, Anatolia, the Levant, Cyprus, and the Aegean lay in ruins, but human resilience would gradually forge new pathways from these ashes.

"The collapse of Bronze Age civilization was not merely an ending," writes archaeologist Susan Sherratt, "but rather a complex transformation that created the conditions for new social, political, and economic arrangements to emerge" (Sherratt 2003: 37). This transformation—occurring at different rates and in different forms across the region—would ultimately lead to the diverse mosaic of Iron Age cultures that formed the foundation of classical Mediterranean civilization.

Regional Transformations: A Fragmented Landscape

Egypt, though weakened, maintained its territorial integrity and cultural continuity through the collapse (Shaw 2000). The New Kingdom eventually gave way to the Third Intermediate Period (c. 1069-664 BCE), characterized by political fragmentation but continued cultural vitality. While Egyptian influence in the Levant diminished significantly, the core of Egyptian civilization persisted along the Nile Valley.

The Hittite Empire, conversely, disappeared completely as a political entity. In its Anatolian heartland, smaller Neo-Hittite kingdoms emerged after a significant period of demographic decline and political reorganization (Hawkins 2000). These successor states—such as Carchemish, Tabal, and Que—preserved elements of Hittite culture, including hieroglyphic Luwian writing and artistic traditions, while developing new political structures on a more modest scale.

Cyprus experienced substantial disruption but remarkable cultural continuity (Karageorghis 1992). After a period of abandonment at several major centers, new settlements emerged that maintained aspects of Late Bronze Age Cypriot culture while incorporating Aegean elements. The island's crucial role in Mediterranean metallurgy would continue through the Early Iron Age, though within new economic networks.

In Greece, the collapse of Mycenaean palatial civilization led to a dramatic simplification of material culture and political organization (Dickinson 2006). The so-called "Greek Dark Age" (c. 1100-800 BCE) saw population decline, the loss of writing, and reduced architectural complexity. Yet even during this period, communities maintained important cultural traditions that would later contribute to the emergence of Archaic Greek civilization.

Perhaps the most dramatic transformations occurred in the Levant, where the collapse of Egyptian imperial control and Hittite influence created opportunities for new political formations. The vacuum left by these imperial powers allowed for the emergence of diverse polities including Phoenician city-states, Aramean kingdoms, and Philistine settlements along the southern coastal plain.

Phoenicians: Maritime Innovators

Among the most significant post-collapse developments was the rise of Phoenician city-states along the central Levantine coast (Bell 2006). Centers like Tyre, Sidon, and Byblos—which had existed as Bronze Age trading hubs—emerged from the collapse with renewed independence and maritime focus.

"The Phoenicians represent one of the clearest examples of cultural and economic continuity through the collapse period," notes archaeologist Carolina López-Ruiz. "They preserved Bronze Age Canaanite traditions while innovating in response to new conditions, particularly in maritime trade and colonization" (cited in Broodbank 2013: 445).

Archaeological evidence from Phoenician centers shows minimal disruption compared to other regions. At Sarepta, for instance, pottery traditions show gradual evolution rather than abrupt change. The Phoenicians maintained writing through the collapse period, eventually developing the alphabetic script that would become the foundation for Greek, Latin, and numerous other writing systems.

By the 10th-9th centuries BCE, Phoenician maritime activities had expanded dramatically, establishing colonies and trading posts throughout the Mediterranean. Their commercial networks helped reconnect the fragmented post-collapse world, facilitating the spread of technologies, artistic styles, and ideas across the region.

Neo-Hittite Kingdoms: Cultural Persistence

In southeastern Anatolia and northern Syria, several Neo-Hittite kingdoms emerged from the ashes of the Hittite Empire (Weeden 2013). Archaeological work at sites like Carchemish, Tell Tayinat, and Zincirli reveals how these polities maintained elements of Hittite imperial culture while adapting to new political realities.

The discovery of monumental architecture and hieroglyphic Luwian inscriptions at these sites demonstrates cultural continuity despite political fragmentation (Hawkins 2000). At Carchemish, for example, rulers continued to use Hittite royal titles and artistic conventions centuries after the fall of Hattusa.

These kingdoms operated on a smaller scale than their imperial predecessor, focusing on regional trade and local resource exploitation rather than long-distance exchange. Their mixed cultural character—combining Hittite, Hurrian, Aramean, and local elements—reflects the fluid, multicultural environment of the post-collapse Levant.

Israel and Judah: Emerging Kingdoms

The collapse period also witnessed the gradual emergence of the kingdoms of Israel and Judah in the central and southern Levant (Finkelstein 2002). Archaeological evidence suggests these polities developed from local Canaanite populations rather than through external invasion, though the process remains debated.

Early Iron Age highland villages in the region show evidence of increasing social complexity and economic specialization through the 11th and 10th centuries BCE (Master 2001). By the 9th century BCE, clear evidence of state formation appears, including monumental architecture, administrative systems, and distinctive material culture.

The relationship between these emerging states and their neighbors—particularly the Philistines to the west—would shape much of the region's subsequent history and features prominently in biblical narratives.

The Philistine Phenomenon: Newcomers in Canaan

Among the most archaeologically visible post-collapse developments was the emergence of Philistine culture in the southern coastal plain of Canaan (Yasur-Landau 2010). Unlike some other post-collapse formations, the Philistines represent clear evidence of population movement and settlement by groups associated with the Sea Peoples migrations.

Egyptian texts from Medinet Habu explicitly mention the defeat and subsequent settlement of the Peleset (Philistines) in the region: "I settled them in strongholds, bound in my name. Their military classes were as numerous as hundred-thousands. I assigned portions for them all with clothing and provisions from the treasuries and granaries each year" (Kitchen 1996: 22).

While the Egyptian account suggests controlled resettlement of captives, the archaeological reality appears more complex. Evidence from key sites like Ashdod, Ashkelon, Ekron, Gath, and Tel Miqne reveals a distinctive material culture that combines Aegean elements with local Canaanite traditions and Egyptian influences (Killebrew 2005).

Arrival and Initial Settlement

The timing of the Philistine arrival remains subject to debate, with most scholars placing it in the early 12th century BCE. Lawrence Stager of Harvard University, based on his excavations at Ashkelon, identified what he termed an "immigration horizon"—a stratigraphic layer marking the initial Philistine settlement—dating to approximately 1175 BCE (Stager 1995).

This timing aligns with Ramesses III's account of his victory over the Sea Peoples around 1180-1175 BCE and subsequent settlement of captives. However, some scholars, including Israel Finkelstein, have proposed a "low chronology" that would place the main Philistine settlement phase somewhat later, around 1140-1130 BCE (Finkelstein 2000).

The pattern of settlement shows clear strategic consideration. The five major Philistine centers—the Pentapolis mentioned in biblical texts—were positioned along key trade routes connecting Egypt with the Levantine interior and beyond. This positioning suggests the Philistines quickly recognized and exploited the economic potential of their new territory.

Archaeological evidence indicates that the initial Philistine settlement involved some violence and destruction at existing Canaanite sites. At Ashdod, for example, excavators identified a destruction layer followed immediately by the appearance of early Philistine pottery (Dothan 1982). However, the pattern varies significantly between sites, suggesting a complex process of conquest, accommodation, and integration rather than uniform violent takeover.

Philistine Material Culture: A Distinctive Assemblage

The most archaeologically visible aspect of Philistine identity is their distinctive pottery tradition, particularly the style known as Philistine Bichrome ware. This pottery combines decorative elements clearly derived from Mycenaean traditions with local Canaanite forms and production techniques (Killebrew 1998).

Trude Dothan, the pioneering archaeologist of Philistine culture, described this pottery as "the calling card of the Philistines," noting that its distribution closely matches the territory associated with Philistine settlement in textual sources (Dothan 1982: 219). The distinctive decorative motifs—including birds, spirals, and checkerboard patterns—show clear parallels with Late Helladic IIIC pottery from the Aegean, supporting the connection between the Philistines and Aegean populations.

Analysis of this pottery reveals a fascinating process of cultural adaptation. Early examples (sometimes called Philistine 1) show the strongest Aegean influences, while later phases (Philistine 2 and 3) demonstrate increasing integration of local Canaanite elements (Maeir, Hitchcock, and Horwitz 2013). This evolution suggests that while the initial settlers maintained strong connections to their Aegean heritage, subsequent generations increasingly adapted to their Levantine environment.

Beyond pottery, Philistine material culture included distinctive architectural elements. Excavations at Ekron and Ashdod have revealed buildings with hearth rooms and megaron-style plans reminiscent of Aegean architecture (Allen 1994). These structures, typically featuring a long hall with a central hearth and sometimes an antechamber, represent a clear departure from standard Canaanite building traditions.

Cultic practices provide additional evidence of the Philistines' distinctive cultural identity. Excavations at Ekron uncovered a temple complex with features suggesting Aegean-inspired religious practices. Similarly, distinctive female figurines found at Philistine sites bear closer resemblance to Mycenaean and Cypriot examples than to local Canaanite traditions.

Dietary practices further distinguish Philistine settlements from their neighbors. Zooarchaeological studies at Ashkelon and Ekron reveal a significant consumption of pork—a practice uncommon among local Canaanite and later Israelite populations (Stager 1991). Seiji Shibata's analysis of faunal remains from Ekron showed that pigs constituted approximately 20% of the meat diet in Philistine contexts, compared to less than 5% in non-Philistine settlements.

The presence of unique cooking vessels, particularly a closed cooking pot different from the open cooking pots typical in Canaanite contexts, suggests distinctive culinary practices (Yasur-Landau 2003). These cooking jugs, suitable for preparing stews and similar dishes, may reflect culinary traditions brought from the Aegean.

Technological Innovation and Economic Adaptation

The Philistines were not merely preservers of Aegean traditions but active innovators who contributed significantly to technological development in the region. Archaeological evidence from Philistine sites reveals advanced metallurgical capabilities, sophisticated textile production, and innovations in agricultural techniques.

Excavations at Tel Miqne-Ekron uncovered what excavator Seymour Gitin described as "the largest industrial complex for the production of olive oil yet excavated in the ancient Mediterranean world" (cited in Maeir and Hitchcock 2017: 155). Dating to the 7th century BCE, this complex contained over 100 olive oil installations capable of producing an estimated 500 tons of olive oil annually. This industrial-scale production represents a remarkable economic adaptation that made Ekron a major exporter of olive oil in the late Iron Age.

Metallurgical evidence from Philistine sites demonstrates sophisticated bronze working and early adoption of iron technology. At Ashkelon, excavators discovered bronze foundries dating to the early phases of Philistine settlement, while later contexts yielded evidence of iron working (Stager 1995). This technological proficiency may reflect metallurgical knowledge brought from the Aegean, where Late Bronze Age metalworking had reached high levels of sophistication.

Textile production appears to have been another Philistine specialization. Numerous loom weights and spindle whorls have been recovered from Philistine contexts, suggesting extensive textile manufacturing. Biblical texts also associate the Philistines with advanced textile work, particularly in the production of dyed fabrics.

From Foreigners to Locals: The Transformation of Philistine Identity

Perhaps the most fascinating aspect of the Philistine phenomenon is the gradual transformation of their cultural identity over time. The archaeological record shows a clear evolution from a distinctly foreign material culture in the 12th century BCE to an increasingly localized but still distinctive culture by the 8th-7th centuries BCE (Yasur-Landau 2012).

This transformation is particularly visible in pottery development. The strongly Aegean-influenced Philistine Bichrome ware of the 12th-11th centuries gradually gave way to more localized forms, though certain decorative elements persisted. By the 8th century BCE, Philistine pottery, while still distinctive, showed significant convergence with broader Levantine ceramic traditions.

Linguistic evidence suggests a similar pattern of cultural integration. While the original language of the Philistines remains unknown (though likely Indo-European based on personal names), inscriptions from later Philistine contexts are written in a local Semitic language using scripts common throughout the region. This linguistic shift suggests that within a few generations, the Philistines had adopted local Canaanite languages while maintaining other aspects of their cultural identity.

Religious practices show a complex pattern of syncretism and adaptation. Early cultic assemblages show strong Aegean influences, but over time, Philistine religion incorporated local Canaanite deities. The discovery of a 7th century BCE inscription at Ekron mentioning "Ptgyh, the lady of Ekron" demonstrates how Philistine religion had developed its own distinctive pantheon combining various cultural elements.

Seymour Gitin, based on his excavations at Ekron, described this process as "acculturation without assimilation"—the Philistines adapted to their Levantine environment while maintaining a distinct cultural identity throughout the Iron Age (cited in Maeir and Hitchcock 2017: 158).

Recent genetic studies have provided new insights into this process of cultural transformation. DNA analysis of human remains from Ashkelon, published in 2019 by a team led by Michal Feldman, demonstrated that the early Philistine population included individuals with genetic ancestry from southern Europe (Feldman et al. 2019). However, within a few generations, this European genetic signature had been largely diluted through intermarriage with local populations, even as distinctive aspects of Philistine material culture persisted.

This genetic evidence aligns remarkably well with the archaeological record, suggesting that Philistine identity was primarily cultural rather than strictly ethnic or biological. The maintenance of distinctive cultural practices despite genetic admixture indicates the importance of cultural transmission and identity formation in the Philistine community.

Political Organization and International Relations

The political organization of Philistine territory evolved significantly over the centuries of their presence in the southern Levant. Biblical texts describe a confederation of five major cities—Gaza, Ashkelon, Ashdod, Ekron, and Gath—each governed by a leader called a seren (plural seranim). This pentapolis structure appears to have been established early in the Philistine settlement period and persisted with modifications through much of the Iron Age.

Archaeological evidence from these major centers confirms their importance as political and economic hubs. Each city developed substantial fortifications, public buildings, and evidence of administrative systems. The relative independence of these centers, combined with evidence of coordination between them, supports the biblical description of a loose confederation rather than a unified state.

The Philistines' relationships with neighboring powers fluctuated dramatically over time. During the 12th-11th centuries BCE, they expanded their influence inland, coming into conflict with emerging Israelite settlements in the highlands. Biblical narratives of conflict between Philistines and Israelites during this period align with archaeological evidence of Philistine material culture at inland sites beyond their core coastal territory.

By the 10th-9th centuries BCE, Philistine expansion had been checked by the rise of the Israelite monarchy. Archaeological evidence from Gath (Tell es-Safi) shows that this important Philistine center was destroyed in the late 9th century BCE, likely by Aramean forces under Hazael of Damascus, as mentioned in 2 Kings 12:17 (Maeir et al. 2013).

The 8th-7th centuries BCE saw the Philistine cities increasingly drawn into the imperial politics of the Neo-Assyrian and later Neo-Babylonian empires. Assyrian records mention Philistine rulers as both rebels and vassals (Kuhrt 1995). The Assyrian king Sargon II depicted the conquest of Philistine Ashdod on palace reliefs at Khorsabad, while royal inscriptions record tribute from Philistine cities.

Despite these imperial entanglements, archaeological evidence demonstrates that the Philistine cities maintained considerable prosperity and cultural distinctiveness under Assyrian domination. Ekron, in particular, reached its peak of economic power during the 7th century BCE as a major producer of olive oil within the Assyrian economic sphere (Gitin et al. 1998).

The end of the Philistine political presence came with the Babylonian campaigns in the region during the late 7th and early 6th centuries BCE. Archaeological evidence from Ashkelon shows dramatic destruction by Babylonian forces under Nebuchadnezzar II in 604 BCE, a campaign also documented in Babylonian chronicles (Stager 1996). While some Philistine cultural elements persisted in the region after this period, the distinctive political entities of the Philistine pentapolis had effectively come to an end.

Cultural Legacy and Historical Significance

The significance of the Philistines extends far beyond their relatively brief political florescence in the southern Levant. As one of the most archaeologically visible examples of population movement and cultural adaptation following the Bronze Age collapse, they provide crucial insights into processes of migration, settlement, and identity formation in the ancient Mediterranean (Barako 2000).

The Philistine case demonstrates how immigrant groups could successfully establish themselves in new territories during periods of systemic collapse, adapting their cultural practices to new environments while maintaining distinctive identities. Their ability to synthesize Aegean traditions with local Canaanite elements and Egyptian influences resulted in a unique cultural complex that contributed significantly to the multicultural environment of the Iron Age Levant.

Technologically, the Philistines appear to have played an important role in the transmission and development of innovations including iron working, specialized olive oil production, and textile manufacturing. Their strategic position along major trade routes facilitated cultural and technological exchange between Egypt, the Levant, and the wider Mediterranean world.

The Philistine phenomenon also illustrates the complex relationship between material culture, ethnicity, and identity in the ancient world. The persistence of distinctive Philistine cultural practices despite genetic admixture with local populations demonstrates how cultural identity could be maintained through social practices, material traditions, and collective memory rather than strict biological descent.

In the broader context of the post-collapse Mediterranean, the Philistines represent one example of the diverse cultural formations that emerged from the ashes of the Late Bronze Age system. Their contemporaries—including Phoenicians, Neo-Hittites, early Israelites, and others—similarly combined cultural preservation with innovation and adaptation, creating the mosaic of Iron Age societies that would ultimately shape the classical Mediterranean world.

The Wider Transformation: From Bronze to Iron Ages

The Philistine phenomenon occurred within the broader context of the transition from the Late Bronze Age to the Early Iron Age—a transformation that reshaped Mediterranean societies at multiple levels (Van De Mieroop 2016). This transition involved not only changes in material technology but fundamental shifts in political organization, economic systems, and cultural expression.

Perhaps the most significant aspect of this transformation was the shift from palace-centered economies to more diverse and decentralized economic arrangements. The collapse of palatial systems in Greece, Anatolia, and parts of the Levant created opportunities for new economic actors and institutions to emerge.

In Greece, the disappearance of Mycenaean palaces led to a period of reduced social complexity before the gradual emergence of the polis system. In the Levant, the decline of Egyptian imperial control and the destruction of palace centers like Ugarit created space for more entrepreneurial forms of trade and production, exemplified by Phoenician commercial ventures and Philistine industrial innovations.

Significant changes in social organization accompanied this economic transformation. The highly stratified palace societies of the Late Bronze Age gave way to more diverse social arrangements in the Early Iron Age. While elites certainly persisted, their power was often based on different foundations, requiring new forms of legitimation and expression.

Cultural expression also underwent significant transformation. The internationalism of Late Bronze Age elite culture—characterized by shared luxury goods, artistic conventions, and diplomatic practices across diverse regions—gave way to more localized cultural expressions in the Early Iron Age (Feldman 2006). These local traditions, however, often incorporated and adapted elements from the cosmopolitan Bronze Age world rather than representing complete breaks with the past.

The period also saw important technological transitions, most notably the gradual adoption of iron technology. While the "Iron Age" name suggests a revolutionary change in metal technology, the actual transition was gradual and uneven. Bronze remained important for many applications, while iron technology developed incrementally over several centuries.

The Philistines appear to have been early adopters of iron technology in the Levant, though not its initial introducers. Excavations at Philistine sites have yielded iron artifacts from early settlement phases, becoming more common in later periods. This technological adaptation reflects the Philistines' general pattern of innovation and synthesis.

Perhaps most fundamentally, the Bronze Age-Iron Age transition involved a reconfiguration of connectivity across the Mediterranean. The integrated international system of the Late Bronze Age, with its diplomatic networks and palace-sponsored trade, collapsed. In its place, new forms of connectivity gradually emerged, often driven by different actors and operating according to different principles. Phoenician maritime expansion, Greek colonial ventures, and Philistine participation in regional trade networks all contributed to the reconstitution of Mediterranean connectivity during the Early Iron Age.

This new connectivity, less centralized and more commercially driven than its Bronze Age predecessor, would ultimately extend further and penetrate deeper than the earlier system, laying foundations for the intensive Mediterranean integration of the classical period.

Conclusion: The Philistines in Mediterranean Perspective

The Philistine phenomenon offers a remarkable case study in cultural resilience, adaptation, and transformation following systemic collapse (Hitchcock and Maeir 2014). Arriving in the southern Levant amid the disruptions of the late

13th and early 12th centuries BCE, these migrants—likely including significant populations from the Aegean—established a distinctive cultural presence that would persist for over six centuries.

Their success stemmed not from isolation or resistance to change, but from their capacity for cultural synthesis and innovation. Combining elements of their Aegean heritage with local Canaanite traditions and influences from neighboring powers like Egypt, the Philistines created a dynamic cultural complex that continuously evolved while maintaining its distinctive character.

The archaeological record of Philistine settlement reveals a process of "becoming local while staying foreign"—a delicate balance of adaptation and preservation that allowed them to thrive in their new environment while maintaining a clear sense of distinctive identity.

This process involved not only material culture but social practices, culinary traditions, religious beliefs, and economic specializations.

In the broader context of post-collapse transformations, the Philistines represent one of several new cultural formations that emerged from the ashes of the Late Bronze Age system. Together with Phoenicians, Neo-Hittites, early Israelites, and others, they contributed to the rich cultural mosaic of the Iron Age Mediterranean—a world of greater diversity but also new forms of connectivity and exchange.

The legacy of these post-collapse innovations would prove enduring. The alphabetic writing system developed by the Phoenicians, the religious traditions of Israel and Judah, the commercial networks pioneered by various Mediterranean groups, and the technological advances of the early Iron Age all contributed foundations for subsequent Mediterranean civilizations.

The Sea Peoples migrations, including the movement that brought the Philistines to Canaan, thus represent not merely a destructive conclusion to the Bronze Age world but a transformative episode that helped shape the Mediterranean's future. From the ashes of collapse emerged new possibilities—cultural innovations, political experiments, and social arrangements that would define the region for centuries to come.

As we examine the archaeological evidence of these ancient transformations, we gain insight not only into a fascinating historical period but into broader patterns of human resilience and adaptation in the face of systemic change. The Philistines and their contemporaries remind us that periods of collapse, while undeniably traumatic, can also create openings for innovation, cultural synthesis, and the emergence of new social forms—lessons perhaps relevant to our own era of rapid change and systemic challenges.

Chapter 7

The "Dark Age" and Rebirth

Iron Age Transformation and Legacy

The transition from the Late Bronze Age to the Early Iron Age in the eastern Mediterranean was not merely a change in metallurgical technology, but a profound transformation in political organization, economic systems, and cultural expressions (Van De Mieroop 2016). The period following the Sea Peoples' movements witnessed the emergence of a fundamentally different world—one characterized by fragmentation, localization, and eventual innovation.

Fragmentation and Decentralization: The Iron Age I Landscape

The collapse of the integrated Bronze Age system left a political vacuum across much of the eastern Mediterranean. Where once stood powerful, centralized kingdoms with extensive bureaucracies and international diplomatic networks, the Iron Age I (roughly 1200-1000 BCE) witnessed a patchwork of smaller political entities with more limited territorial control (Middleton 2017).

"The collapse of Bronze Age civilizations created a political landscape resembling a shattered mosaic," wrote Itamar Singer in his seminal work on the period. "Where once stood cohesive kingdoms with clear hierarchies and established borders, we now find a proliferation of smaller polities operating according to different organizational principles" (Singer 1999: 603).

This political fragmentation is evident in settlement patterns across the region. In Greece, the elaborate palaces that had dominated the Mycenaean landscape were abandoned, replaced by smaller, simpler settlements lacking monumental architecture (Dickinson 2006). The Linear B administrative script disappeared entirely, suggesting the collapse of the bureaucratic systems it had served. As archaeologist Anthony Snodgrass observed, "The post-Mycenaean world was one of dramatically reduced scale and complexity, with political organization retreating to the level of individual villages or small regional groupings" (cited in Middleton 2010: 89).

In Anatolia, the vacuum left by the Hittite Empire's collapse was filled by numerous smaller states. The Neo-Hittite kingdoms that emerged in southeastern Anatolia and northern Syria preserved elements of Hittite political culture and iconography but operated on a fraction of the imperial scale (Hawkins 2000).

Cities like Carchemish and Malatya became centers of these successor states, each controlling relatively limited territories compared to their imperial predecessor.

The Levant experienced similar fragmentation. The Egyptian withdrawal from its imperial possessions in Canaan created opportunities for local political formations to emerge (Redford 1992). The Philistine pentapolis (five cities) in the southern coastal plain represented one such development, while inland regions saw the gradual emergence of territorial states including early Israel, Ammon, Moab, and Edom. In the northern Levant, city-states like Byblos, Sidon, and Tyre—later known collectively as Phoenicia—operated independently, though often maintaining trade relationships with each other (Bell 2006).

Economic localization accompanied this political decentralization. The elaborate palace-centered economies of the Late Bronze Age, with their centralized collection and redistribution of resources, gave way to more diverse and localized economic arrangements (Sherratt 2003). Long-distance trade continued but operated according to different principles and often involved different actors.

Archaeological evidence from across the region demonstrates this economic transformation. The uniformity of ceramic traditions that had characterized the Late Bronze Age international style gave way to more localized pottery traditions. Trade in luxury goods declined significantly, with prestige items like Egyptian scarabs and Mycenaean pictorial pottery becoming much rarer in Early Iron Age contexts (Feldman 2006). The standardized weight systems that had facilitated international commerce became more varied and localized.

Cyprus, which had been a crucial node in Late Bronze Age metal trade networks, experienced significant disruption but also remarkable continuity (Knapp 2013). The island's economy contracted, with several coastal sites abandoned, but others continued to function. As archaeological excavations at Kition and other sites have shown, metalworking activities continued, though oriented more toward regional than international markets.

The island of Sardinia, at the western edge of the Bronze Age Mediterranean network, experienced a different trajectory. The indigenous Nuragic culture underwent significant transformation during this period, with increased fortification of settlements suggesting heightened concerns about security (Vagnetti 2000). However, connections with the eastern Mediterranean continued, albeit in altered form. Cypriot-style bronze stands and other eastern Mediterranean influences appear in Sardinian contexts of the early Iron Age, suggesting that some form of connectivity persisted despite systemic collapse elsewhere.

This pattern of fragmentation and localization did not mean complete isolation, however. Archaeological evidence indicates that various forms of interregional contact continued throughout the Iron Age I period, though operating through different mechanisms than the palace-sponsored trade of the Late Bronze Age (Monroe 2009). Small-scale maritime commerce, population movements, and the transmission of ideas and technologies continued to connect different parts of the Mediterranean basin, laying foundations for the more intensive connectivity that would emerge in subsequent centuries.

As Assaf Yasur-Landau has argued, "The Early Iron Age witnessed not the end of Mediterranean connectivity but its reconfiguration. New actors, new routes, and new commodities emerged, creating networks that were in some ways more resilient than their Bronze Age predecessors precisely because they were less dependent on centralized political structures" (Yasur-Landau 2010: 234).

The material culture of the period reflects both fragmentation and continued connectivity. While pottery styles became more regionalized, technological innovations like iron working spread gradually across the Mediterranean. Textile production techniques, architectural forms, and culinary practices show both local development and interregional influences. Writing systems diversified, with the Phoenician alphabet emerging as a simpler alternative to the complex scripts of the Bronze Age, eventually spreading widely throughout the Mediterranean.

This period of fragmentation and localization, while often characterized as a "dark age" in older scholarship, is increasingly recognized as a time of important cultural and technological innovation (Wengrow 2010). The reduced scale of political organization created spaces for experimentation and adaptation that would have significant long-term consequences for Mediterranean history.

The Long Shadow: Sea Peoples' Impact on Historical Development

The movements of the Sea Peoples and the systemic collapse they took part in had profound and lasting impacts on Mediterranean historical development (Cline 2014). These effects manifested not only in the immediate aftermath of collapse but continued to shape political, cultural, and economic patterns for centuries afterward.

Perhaps the most direct long-term impact was the establishment of Philistine culture in the southern Levant. The archaeological record reveals that Philistine material culture, while gradually incorporating more local elements, maintained its distinctive character for over six centuries (Yasur-Landau 2012). Their five major cities—Gaza, Ashkelon, Ashdod, Ekron, and Gath—remained important urban centers throughout the Iron Age, with Ekron developing into a major center of olive oil production by the 7th century BCE (Gitin et al. 1998).

The Philistine presence had significant implications for the development of neighboring peoples, particularly the emerging Israelites. Biblical texts portray the Philistines as Israel's primary antagonists during the early monarchy period, and while these accounts contain later literary elaborations, they likely reflect genuine historical conflicts over territory and resources. As Lawrence Stager observed, "The geographic position of Philistia, controlling coastal plains and key inland routes, placed them in natural competition with highland populations for economic and political dominance in the region" (Stager 1995: 332).

This conflict may have sped up the political consolidation of early Israel. The biblical narrative presents the Philistine threat as a key factor motivating the establishment of the Israelite monarchy under Saul and David. While archaeological evidence for a unified Israelite state in the 10th century BCE remains contested (Finkelstein 2002), the presence of a powerful and culturally distinct neighbor along the coastal plain certainly influenced political developments in the central highlands.

The Philistines also served as important cultural intermediaries. Their connections to Aegean traditions and continued maritime orientation positioned them to facilitate the transmission of ideas, technologies, and artistic styles between the eastern Mediterranean and the Levant (Barako 2000). Archaeological evidence from Philistine sites shows ongoing connections with Cyprus and the Aegean throughout the Iron Age, providing channels for cultural exchange even during periods of political fragmentation.

Beyond the specific case of the Philistines, the Sea Peoples movements contributed to a broader reconfiguration of Mediterranean populations and cultural geography. The disruptions of the late 13th and early 12th centuries BCE created conditions for significant population movements and the establishment of new cultural formations across the region.

In Cyprus, the post-collapse period saw the emergence of new settlement patterns and cultural expressions. Sites like Kition show evidence of new cultural elements appearing alongside indigenous traditions, suggesting the arrival of new populations, possibly including groups associated with the Sea Peoples (Karageorghis 1992). These demographic changes contributed to the island's distinctive Iron Age culture, which combined Cypriot, Levantine, and Aegean elements.

In the western Mediterranean, the disruptions of the Late Bronze Age collapse may have accelerated processes of cultural interaction and hybridization. Sardinia's Nuragic culture shows increased evidence of eastern Mediterranean influences in the early Iron Age, while Sicily and southern Italy witnessed complex interactions between indigenous populations and maritime traders from the eastern Mediterranean (Jung 2018). These processes laid foundations for the intensive cultural interactions of the later Iron Age and Archaic period.

The collapse of the Hittite Empire and the weakening of Egyptian power in the Levant created a geopolitical reconfiguration with lasting consequences. The power vacuum in northern Syria and southeastern Anatolia allowed for the emergence of the Neo-Hittite states and Aramean kingdoms, which would play important roles in the political landscape of the early first millennium BCE (Weeden 2013). These states preserved elements of Hittite political culture and iconography while developing distinctive new features.

In the northern Levant, the collapse of Bronze Age imperial systems created conditions for the flourishing of Phoenician city-states. Cities like Tyre, Sidon, and Byblos, which had been subordinate to Egyptian or Hittite power during much of the Late Bronze Age, emerged as independent political entities with distinctive cultural identities. Their maritime orientation and commercial expertise, developed in part as an adaptation to post-collapse conditions, would position them to play crucial roles in subsequent Mediterranean history.

The Sea Peoples movements also contributed to significant technological transitions. While they did not introduce iron technology, as once believed, the disruptions they participated in accelerated the transition from bronze to iron as the dominant metallurgical technology. The collapse of the international trading networks that had supplied copper and tin for bronze production created incentives to develop iron technology, which relied on more widely available resources.

As archaeologist James Muhly noted, "The Bronze Age collapse disrupted the complex procurement networks required for bronze production, creating conditions that favored the development of iron technology despite its initial technical limitations" (cited in Sherratt 2003: 52). This technological shift had profound long-term implications, eventually enabling more widespread access to metal tools and weapons than had been possible under the more centralized bronze production systems.

Perhaps most fundamentally, the Sea Peoples movements and the Bronze Age collapse they participated in marked a crucial transition in Mediterranean historical development. The destruction of the palace-centered political and economic systems of the Late Bronze Age created openings for new forms of social and political organization to emerge. The more decentralized Iron Age world, while initially less complex in some respects, ultimately proved more resilient and adaptable than its Bronze Age predecessor.

As historian Carol Bell has observed, "The collapse of Bronze Age civilizations, catastrophic as it was for contemporary populations, created conditions for innovations that would have been difficult or impossible within the rigid hierarchies of the palace systems. The fragmentation of the 12th century BCE, viewed in long-term perspective, appears less as an ending than as a crucial transition toward new forms of Mediterranean connectivity" (Bell 2006: 187).

From Ashes to Kingdoms: The Rise of Iron Age States

The political fragmentation that characterized the early Iron Age did not persist indefinitely. Beginning in the 10th century BCE and accelerating in the 9th and 8th centuries, new territorial states emerged across the eastern Mediterranean, building on the foundations laid during the post-collapse period (Kuhrt 1995).

In the southern Levant, the biblical narrative describes the establishment of a unified Israelite monarchy under David and Solomon in the 10th century BCE, followed by its division into the northern kingdom of Israel and southern kingdom of Judah. While the archaeological evidence for a unified monarchy remains contested, with minimalist scholars questioning its historical existence or extent (Finkelstein 2002), there is clear evidence for state formation processes in the region during this period.

The kingdom of Israel, with its capital eventually established at Samaria, emerged as a significant regional power in the 9th century BCE under the Omride dynasty. Archaeological excavations at Samaria, Jezreel, Hazor, and Megiddo reveal substantial public architecture, fortification systems, and administrative structures indicating a developed state apparatus (Master 2001). The Mesha Stele, erected by the king of Moab around 840 BCE, provides extrabiblical confirmation of Israel's territorial expansion under the Omrides, describing how King Omri "had oppressed Moab for many days."

The smaller kingdom of Judah, centered on Jerusalem, developed more gradually. Archaeological evidence indicates that Jerusalem remained a relatively modest settlement until the late 8th century BCE, when it experienced significant expansion (Finkelstein 2002). This growth coincided with the destruction of the northern kingdom of Israel by Assyria in 722 BCE, suggesting that refugees from the north may have contributed to Judah's development. By the 7th century BCE, Judah had emerged as a fully developed state with a complex administrative system, as evidenced by the distribution of standardized storage jars bearing official seal impressions (lmlk seals) and the presence of a sophisticated scribal tradition.

Both indigenous traditions and external models influenced the development of these Israelite states. The biblical narrative presents kingship as a foreign institution adopted in response to external threats, particularly from the Philistines. While this account contains theological perspectives on monarchy, it may reflect historical memory of how state formation was accelerated by competition with more developed neighbors.

Further north, the Phoenician city-states of Tyre, Sidon, and Byblos pursued a different developmental path. Rather than expanding territorially, these coastal cities intensified their maritime commercial activities, establishing trading networks that eventually extended throughout the Mediterranean (Bell 2006). By the 9th century BCE, Phoenician merchants had established outposts in Cyprus, North Africa, Sicily, Sardinia, and Spain, creating an extensive commercial network that would profoundly influence Mediterranean development.

The archaeological record reveals the extent of this Phoenician expansion. At Carthage in North Africa, founded according to tradition by colonists from Tyre around 814 BCE, excavations have uncovered Phoenician material culture dating to the late 9th century BCE. Similar evidence appears at sites across the central and western Mediterranean, indicating the establishment of a commercial network of unprecedented scale and reach.

Significant cultural diffusion accompanied Phoenician commercial expansion. Perhaps most importantly, the Phoenician alphabetic writing system—a simplified alternative to the complex scripts of the Bronze Age—spread widely throughout the Mediterranean. Greeks adapted this system to create their own alphabet, adding vowel notation, while Etruscans and eventually Romans developed their own alphabetic scripts based ultimately on Phoenician models. This technological diffusion had profound implications for literacy, administration, and cultural development across the Mediterranean world.

In northern Syria and southeastern Anatolia, the Neo-Hittite states that emerged following the Hittite Empire's collapse developed into substantial regional powers during the early first millennium BCE (Hawkins 2000). States centered on cities like Carchemish, Malatya, and Sam'al preserved elements of Hittite political culture and artistic traditions while incorporating new influences, particularly from Aramean populations that had become increasingly prominent in the region.

The material culture of these Neo-Hittite states demonstrates this cultural synthesis. Monumental architecture and relief sculptures continue Hittite artistic traditions while incorporating new elements (Weeden 2013). Bilingual inscriptions in Luwian hieroglyphs and Aramaic reflect the linguistic diversity of these states and their position at the intersection of different cultural traditions.

Further east, the Aramean states that emerged in Syria represented another important post-collapse development. Centered on cities like Damascus and Hamath, dynasties that claimed Aramean ethnic identity ruled these states, though their populations and cultural expressions were typically mixed. By the 9th century BCE, Aramean states had become significant regional powers, engaging diplomatically and militarily with Assyria, Israel, and other neighboring states.

The Aramean cultural and linguistic influence extended far beyond their political boundaries. The Aramaic language, written in an alphabetic script derived from Phoenician, gradually emerged as a lingua franca for international communication across the Near East. By the 8th century BCE, Aramaic was being used for administration in the Neo-Assyrian Empire, beginning a period of linguistic prominence that would continue under Persian rule and beyond.

The rise of these various Iron Age states was not an isolated process but occurred within a broader context of increasing interregional connectivity. Archaeological evidence indicates growing commercial exchange across the Mediterranean during the 9th and 8th centuries BCE (Broodbank 2013). Greek pottery appears in increasing quantities at sites in the Levant, North Africa, and Italy, while Phoenician goods are found throughout the Mediterranean basin. This commercial integration created conditions for cultural exchange on an unprecedented scale, with artistic styles, technologies, and ideas traveling alongside material goods.

The emerging Iron Age states also operated within an increasingly interconnected diplomatic system. The biblical account of Solomon's diplomatic marriage to a "daughter of Pharaoh" may reflect historical memory of such international relationships, while extrabiblical sources like the Amarna letters provide direct evidence of diplomatic exchanges between various regional powers (Moran 1992).

By the late 8th century BCE, however, this system of multiple regional states was increasingly overshadowed by the expansion of the Neo-Assyrian Empire (Kuhrt 1995). Under rulers like Tiglath-Pileser III (745-727 BCE), Shalmaneser V (726-722 BCE), and Sargon II (721-705 BCE), Assyria extended its control across the Near East, incorporating many of the states that had emerged in the post-collapse period.

The kingdom of Israel fell to Assyria in 722 BCE, with large portions of its population deported and replaced by settlers from other parts of the empire—a standard Assyrian practice designed to prevent rebellion. The Phoenician cities and Neo-Hittite states were gradually reduced to vassal status or directly incorporated into Assyrian provincial administration. Only Egypt and some states on the imperial periphery, including Judah, maintained independence, though often as tribute-paying vassals.

This Assyrian imperial expansion represented a partial return to the political centralization of the Bronze Age, though operating according to different principles and on an even larger scale. The Assyrian Empire developed sophisticated administrative systems for controlling its vast territories, including provincial organization, standardized taxation, road networks, and communication systems. These imperial innovations would influence subsequent empires, including the Neo-Babylonian, Persian, and eventually Hellenistic states.

Yet even as political centralization returned under Assyrian imperialism, the cultural and technological innovations of the post-collapse period continued to develop. Iron technology became increasingly sophisticated, with new production techniques allowing for harder and more versatile metal tools and weapons. Alphabetic writing systems spread more widely, gradually replacing the complex scripts of the Bronze Age and enabling broader literacy. Commercial networks continued to expand, now often operating within imperial frameworks rather than between independent states.

The Sea Peoples, who had participated in the destruction of the Bronze Age system four centuries earlier, would have been unrecognizable in this new world. Yet the processes they had set in motion—political reconfiguration, population movements, cultural hybridization, and technological adaptation—continued to shape Mediterranean development long after their direct influence had faded.

As archaeologist Ann Killebrew has observed, "The Sea Peoples were not merely destroyers of an old order but unwitting catalysts for the emergence of new cultural and political formations. The world they helped to create, through destruction and subsequent settlement, laid foundations for developments that would shape Mediterranean history for centuries to come" (Killebrew 2005: 245).

Iron Age Innovations: Technology, Society, and Culture

Significant technological, social, and cultural innovations accompanied the political transformations of the Iron Age, many of which had their roots in adaptations to post-collapse conditions (Wengrow 2010).

Iron technology, which gives the period its name, underwent crucial development during this era. While iron artifacts appear occasionally in Late Bronze Age contexts, the metal was treated primarily as a precious material rather than a practical alternative to bronze. The disruption of bronze supply networks following the collapse created incentives to develop iron working techniques, despite iron's initial technical disadvantages.

Early iron production yielded relatively soft metal, less effective than good-quality bronze for many applications. The crucial innovation came with the development of carburization techniques—the introduction of carbon into iron during the smelting process to create steel. Archaeological evidence from various sites indicates that these techniques were gradually mastered during the early Iron Age, with iron quality improving significantly by the 10th century BCE.

As metallurgist Vagn Buchwald noted, "The transition from bronze to iron represents not merely a change in material but a fundamental shift in metallurgical understanding and practice. Iron working required new technical knowledge, different resources, and alternative production organizations compared to bronze" (cited in Sherratt 2003: 48).

This technological transition had significant social implications. Bronze production had required access to copper and tin sources often separated by considerable distances, necessitating complex procurement networks typically controlled by palace administrations. Iron ore, by contrast, was more widely available, and iron production could be organized on a more local scale. This democratization of metal technology gradually made tools and weapons accessible to broader segments of society.

The Iron Age also witnessed important innovations in agricultural technology. Iron plowshares, more durable and effective than their bronze predecessors, appear in increasing numbers during this period. Terracing techniques were developed or expanded in many Mediterranean regions, allowing cultivation of hillsides previously unsuitable for agriculture (Burke 2008). Water management systems became more sophisticated, with cisterns, channels, and reservoirs constructed to maximize the use of limited water resources.

These agricultural innovations supported population growth and settlement expansion in many regions. In the Israelite highlands, archaeological surveys have documented significant population increase during the Iron Age I and II periods, with numerous new settlements established in previously marginal areas (Finkelstein 1995). Similar patterns appear in parts of Greece, Anatolia, and other Mediterranean regions, suggesting successful adaptation to post-collapse conditions.

Architectural innovations accompanied these demographic changes. New construction techniques developed, often adapted to local materials and conditions. In the Levant, the "four-room house"—a distinctive residential plan with a central courtyard and surrounding rooms—became the standard domestic architecture in Israelite settlements (Stager 1985). In Greece, new temple forms emerged that would eventually develop into the canonical orders of classical architecture. Defensive architecture became increasingly sophisticated, with complex gate systems and casemated walls appearing at many sites.

Transportation technology also advanced during this period. Improvements in shipbuilding techniques enabled more extensive maritime commerce, with specialized merchant vessels developing alongside military ships (Wachsmann 1998). Land transportation benefited from better road construction and the wider use of domesticated equids for traction and riding. The development of the bit and improved harness systems increased the effectiveness of animal traction, while cavalry gradually emerged as a significant military force.

Writing systems underwent crucial transformations during the Iron Age. The complex syllabic scripts of the Bronze Age, which had required specialized scribal training and were used primarily for palace administration, gave way to simpler alphabetic systems. The Phoenician alphabet, with just 22 characters representing consonants, could be learned much more easily than its predecessors. This innovation facilitated wider literacy and new uses of writing beyond administrative record-keeping.

The spread of alphabetic writing had profound cultural implications. In Israel and Judah, it enabled the development of significant literary traditions, including the earliest biblical texts. Inscriptions from this period show that writing was used not only for administration but for personal correspondence, commercial records, religious texts, and commemorative purposes. This expansion of literacy, while still limited compared to modern standards, represented a significant democratization of written culture.

Religious practices also underwent important transformations during the Iron Age. The official state cults of the Bronze Age palace centers gave way to more diverse religious expressions, often with stronger local variations. In Israel and Judah, archaeological evidence indicates a gradual development toward the monotheistic worship of Yahweh, though with significant continuation of other practices including household cults and veneration of Asherah alongside Yahweh.

Material evidence for these religious practices comes from numerous sites. At Kuntillet 'Ajrud in the Sinai, inscriptions mention "Yahweh and his Asherah," suggesting that the divine couple concept remained important in some contexts. Household shrines and figurines, particularly female "pillar figurines" found in Judahite contexts, indicate the importance of domestic religious practices alongside official temple cults.

In Philistia, religious practices combined Aegean elements with local Canaanite influences. Excavations at Ekron uncovered a major temple complex from the 7th century BCE with an inscription dedicating it to "Ptgyh," possibly a goddess with Aegean connections (Gitin et al. 1998). This religious syncretism reflects the Philistines' broader pattern of cultural adaptation and synthesis.

Phoenician religion similarly combined traditional Canaanite elements with innovations. The goddess Astarte gained particular prominence in Phoenician contexts, while the god Melqart became especially associated with Tyre and its colonies. Phoenician religious practices spread with their commercial expansion, influencing religious developments across the Mediterranean.

Artistic traditions also evolved significantly during the Iron Age. In the absence of centralized palace patronage, more diverse regional styles emerged. Phoenician art developed a distinctive aesthetic combining Egyptian, Mesopotamian, and Aegean influences into a sophisticated international style that would be widely imitated (Feldman 2006). Israelite and Judahite art, more constrained by religious prohibitions against certain representations, nonetheless developed distinctive traditions in ivory carving, seal cutting, and architectural decoration.

Philistine art evolved from its initial Aegean-influenced style to incorporate more local elements while maintaining distinctive characteristics. Neo-Hittite art preserved many elements of Hittite imperial iconography while developing new forms and themes. Across the region, artistic production became less centralized and more diverse, though interregional influences remained strong through trade and diplomatic contacts.

Social organization underwent significant transformations during this period. The rigid hierarchies of the palace-centered Bronze Age societies gave way to more varied social structures. While elites remained important, new social groups gained prominence, including merchants operating independently of palace systems, skilled craftspeople serving broader markets, and religious specialists outside palace contexts.

Evidence for these social changes comes from various sources. Settlement patterns show greater diversity, with fewer palace centers and more communities of intermediate size. Burial practices indicate more complex social stratification, with greater variation in grave goods and burial types within communities. Textual evidence, particularly from biblical sources but also from inscriptions, describes social tensions and conflicts between different groups, suggesting a more dynamic social environment than the relatively static hierarchies of the Bronze Age.

Family organization appears to have remained fundamentally patriarchal across most Iron Age societies, though with significant variations in specific practices. Archaeological evidence from domestic contexts indicates that households remained the basic unit of production and consumption in most communities. Extended family compounds appear in many settlements, suggesting that kinship remained a crucial organizing principle despite broader social changes.

These various innovations—technological, social, cultural, and religious—did not develop in isolation but influenced each other in complex ways. Technological changes enabled new social arrangements, which in turn fostered cultural innovations. Religious developments both reflected and shaped social transformations. The resulting cultural systems, while building on Bronze Age foundations, represented novel adaptations to the conditions of the post-collapse world.

As archaeologist William Dever has observed, "The Iron Age societies that emerged from the ashes of Bronze Age collapse were not merely diminished versions of their predecessors but qualitatively different formations. Their innovations—in technology, social organization, religious practice, and cultural expression—would shape Mediterranean history for centuries to come, laying foundations for developments that extend into the classical world and beyond" (cited in Wengrow 2010: 234).

Conclusion: Legacy of Transformation

The Sea Peoples phenomenon, viewed in its broadest historical context, represents a crucial transition point in Mediterranean history (Cline 2014). The movements of these diverse groups, both as raiders and as settlers, participated in and accelerated the collapse of the Late Bronze Age international system. The resulting political fragmentation created conditions for new cultural formations, technological innovations, and social arrangements to emerge during the subsequent Iron Age.

The direct legacy of the Sea Peoples is most clearly visible in the Philistine settlements of the southern Levant. These communities, maintaining distinctive cultural traditions while gradually adapting to local conditions, represented one of several new cultural formations that emerged from the period of collapse and transformation (Yasur-Landau 2010). Their presence influenced the development of neighboring peoples, particularly the Israelites, while their position on important trade routes made them significant participants in the reconstitution of Mediterranean connectivity during the Iron Age.

More broadly, the Sea Peoples movements contributed to a fundamental reconfiguration of Mediterranean cultural geography. The disruption of Bronze Age political systems created openings for new ethnic and cultural identities to emerge or gain prominence. Phoenicians, Israelites, Neo-Hittites, Arameans, and various Greek communities developed distinctive cultural expressions during the early Iron Age, often building on Bronze Age foundations but incorporating significant innovations.

The political fragmentation of the early Iron Age eventually gave way to new forms of integration. The Phoenician commercial network connected distant parts of the Mediterranean through trade rather than imperial control (Bell 2006). The Neo-Assyrian Empire reestablished political centralization across much of the Near East, though operating according to different principles than its Bronze Age predecessors (Kuhrt 1995). Greek colonial expansion created new networks of cultural and commercial exchange in the central and western Mediterranean.

These various processes of fragmentation and reintegration created a Mediterranean world that was simultaneously more diverse and more interconnected than its Bronze Age predecessor (Broodbank 2013). The cultural innovations of the early Iron Age—alphabetic writing, iron technology, new religious concepts, distinctive artistic traditions—spread through these networks of connectivity, influencing developments far beyond their points of origin.

The legacy of these transformations extends well beyond the Iron Age itself. The alphabetic writing systems developed during this period would eventually spread throughout the Mediterranean and beyond, fundamentally changing how information was recorded and transmitted. The religious concepts that emerged in Israel and Judah would develop into Judaism and eventually influence Christianity and Islam. The commercial networks established by Phoenicians and Greeks would create patterns of Mediterranean connectivity that persisted for centuries.

Even the memory of the Sea Peoples themselves became part of this legacy. Egyptian records of their defeat by Ramesses III were preserved and studied by later generations, becoming part of the historical consciousness of subsequent Mediterranean civilizations. Modern archaeological research has recovered material evidence of their movements and settlements, allowing us to reconstruct this crucial episode in Mediterranean history with increasing detail and nuance.

As we examine this evidence, we gain insight not only into a fascinating historical period but into broader patterns of cultural resilience, adaptation, and transformation in the face of systemic change. The Sea Peoples and their contemporaries remind us that periods of collapse, while undeniably traumatic for those experiencing them, can also create openings for innovation, cultural synthesis, and the emergence of new social forms—lessons perhaps relevant to our own era of rapid change and systemic challenges.

Chapter 8

Enduring Mysteries and Modern Interpretations

Interpretive Challenges and New Perspectives

Despite decades of archaeological investigation and scholarly analysis, the Sea Peoples phenomenon continues to present significant interpretive challenges. The fragmentary nature of our evidence—scattered textual references, destruction layers at archaeological sites, stylistic changes in material culture—permits multiple readings and competing narratives (Middleton 2017). As our understanding of Late Bronze Age societies has grown more sophisticated, so too has our appreciation for the complexity of their collapse.

The Question of Origins

Perhaps no aspect of the Sea Peoples phenomenon has generated more scholarly debate than the question of their geographic origins. The Egyptian inscriptions at Medinet Habu name several distinct groups—Peleset, Tjekker, Shekelesh, Denyen, Weshesh, Sherden, Teresh, Lukka, and others—but provide few clear indications of their homelands (Kitchen 1996). Archaeological evidence offers tantalizing but ambiguous clues.

Nancy Sandars, in her pioneering 1978 study The Sea Peoples: Warriors of the Ancient Mediterranean, proposed primarily Aegean origins for many Sea Peoples groups, linking them to the aftermath of Mycenaean collapse. She wrote: "The Sea Peoples were not the cause but the symptom and result of the natural catastrophes and vast economic failures that brought the Bronze Age to an end" (Sandars 1985: 200). This perspective positioned the Sea Peoples primarily as displaced populations seeking new homes after the collapse of their own societies.

Subsequent scholarship has both refined and challenged this view. Trude and Moshe Dothan's influential work on Philistine archaeology strengthened the case for Aegean connections, demonstrating clear links between early Philistine material culture and Mycenaean traditions (Dothan and Dothan 1992). As Trude Dothan observed in The Philistines and Their Material Culture (1982): "The Philistine immigrants brought with them memories of their Aegean homeland expressed in their pottery, architecture, cultic practices, and other aspects of material culture" (Dothan 1982: 295).

However, recent excavations at sites like Tell Tayinat, Tell Afis, and Çineköy in Turkey have revealed settlements with similar "Sea Peoples" material culture in northern Syria and Cilicia (Janeway 2006-2007). These findings have led some scholars to propose more complex models involving multiple points of origin and staged migrations. Archaeologist Ann Killebrew suggests that "rather than representing a single ethnic group, the term 'Sea Peoples' should be understood as a convenient archaeological construct encompassing diverse groups that participated in the complex processes of collapse and regeneration at the end of the Late Bronze Age" (Killebrew 2005: 245).

The specific homelands proposed for individual Sea Peoples groups remain contested:

Archaeologist Eric Cline summarizes the current state of the debate in 1177 B.C.: The Year Civilization Collapsed (2014): "We still do not know for certain where most of these groups came from before they attacked Egypt, despite more than a century of scholarly investigation and speculation. It is probably correct to say that they came from many places rather than one place, which makes their origins even more difficult to pin down" (Cline 2014: 151).

The geographic diversity suggested by these various hypotheses has led many scholars to abandon the search for a single point of origin. Instead, current models often envision the Sea Peoples as heterogeneous coalitions formed through a process of aggregation as displaced groups moved through the Mediterranean, gathering additional participants along the way.

The Question of Identity and Organization

Equally challenging is determining the nature of Sea Peoples identity and social organization. Were they unified confederations with coherent leadership, opportunistic raiders with fluid membership, displaced refugees seeking new homes, or some combination of these? The Egyptian depictions suggest military organization, but may reflect Egyptian conceptions more than Sea Peoples realities (Ben-Dor Evian 2017).

Early scholarship often portrayed the Sea Peoples as coordinated "hordes" or "invaders" operating under unified leadership. This view, influenced by 19th century concepts of migration and invasion, has largely been abandoned in favor of more nuanced models. As archaeologist Susan Sherratt notes: "The 'Sea Peoples' were not a single entity, but rather a convenient term for a variety of different groups of people who were doing different things in different places for different reasons at roughly the same time" (Sherratt 1998: 292).

Several alternative models have emerged:

Archaeologist Assaf Yasur-Landau, in The Philistines and Aegean Migration at the End of the Late Bronze Age (2010), argues for a nuanced approach combining elements of several models: "The migration of the Sea Peoples was neither a single event nor a uniform process. Rather, it comprised multiple movements of diverse groups responding to conditions in their homelands while adapting to circumstances encountered along their journey" (Yasur-Landau 2010: 347).

Material evidence from Philistine settlements suggests that whatever their organization during migration and conflict, at least some Sea Peoples groups established coherent communities with distinctive cultural practices after settlement. These communities maintained certain traditions from their places of origin while adapting to local conditions and gradually integrating with neighboring populations (Killebrew 2005).

The question of identity is further complicated by the likely presence of different social elements within Sea Peoples groups. Egyptian depictions show warriors, women, children, and ox-carts carrying possessions—suggesting family migration rather than purely military movement (Drews 2000). Archaeological evidence from early Philistine sites indicates the presence of craftspeople maintaining specialized production traditions. These diverse social components suggest complex group compositions rather than simple raiding parties.

Climate Change and Systems Collapse

Recent paleoclimate research has significantly advanced our understanding of environmental conditions during the Late Bronze Age collapse, offering new perspectives on the Sea Peoples phenomenon (Kaniewski et al. 2013). Multiple independent climate proxies—including lake sediments, speleothems (cave formations), and deep-sea cores—indicate that the eastern Mediterranean experienced severe drought conditions between approximately 1250-1100 BCE, precisely coinciding with the period of systems collapse and Sea Peoples activity.

Paleoclimatologist David Kaniewski and colleagues, analyzing pollen samples from Syria, identified "a drastic shift to a more arid climate in the Mediterranean and the Middle East" around 1200 BCE (Kaniewski et al. 2013: 8). Similar evidence comes from the Dead Sea, Nile Delta sediments, and caves in Turkey and Israel. This regional climate change appears connected to broader Northern Hemisphere cooling, possibly triggered by volcanic eruptions that affected atmospheric circulation patterns.

The drought's effects would have been particularly severe for Late Bronze Age societies dependent on grain agriculture and specialized production. As archaeologist Brandon Drake observes: "A worst-case scenario would see a decrease in agricultural production due to drought, followed by famine and plague, which would have led to internal strife and collapse of the political system" (cited in Cline 2014: 139). Such conditions could have triggered population movements while simultaneously weakening states' abilities to resist external pressures.

This climate perspective has shifted scholarly understanding of the Sea Peoples from being primarily causes of collapse to being both symptoms and agents of broader systemic failures. The Sea Peoples' movements likely represented responses to deteriorating conditions in their own regions, while their activities further stressed already vulnerable political systems.

However, climate determinism has rightly been rejected by most scholars. As archaeologist A. Bernard Knapp cautions: "Climate change alone cannot explain the complex patterns of societal change evident in the archaeological record. We must consider how environmental stresses interacted with political, economic, and social factors specific to each region and society" (Knapp and Manning 2016: 125).

The systems collapse model, pioneered by Colin Renfrew and refined by scholars like Joseph Tainter and Eric Cline, offers a more comprehensive framework (Middleton 2017). This approach views Late Bronze Age societies as complex systems with multiple interdependencies. In such systems, failures in one component can trigger cascading effects across the network. The Sea Peoples, in this model, represent both a product of initial systemic stresses and an accelerating factor in subsequent collapse.

Technological Transitions

The traditional association between the Sea Peoples and the Bronze-to-Iron transition has undergone significant reassessment. Earlier scholarship often portrayed the Sea Peoples as introducing iron technology, contributing to the military obsolescence of bronze-dependent states. Archaeological evidence has thoroughly disproven this simplistic narrative.

Iron technology developed gradually across the Near East, with early examples appearing well before the Sea Peoples movements. The Hittites had been working with iron since at least the 14th century BCE, though primarily for prestigious rather than practical objects (Muhly 1985). The transition to widespread iron use occurred over centuries following the Bronze Age collapse, driven by multiple factors:

As archaeologist James Muhly notes: "The Sea Peoples did not bring iron technology to the Levant. Rather, they arrived during a period when existing patterns of bronze production were being disrupted, creating conditions that would eventually favor iron adoption" (cited in Sherratt 2003: 52).

In the Philistine case, evidence suggests they initially maintained bronze-working traditions brought from the Aegean, only gradually adopting iron technology in parallel with neighboring populations (Killebrew 2005). Their technological contribution lay not in introducing iron but in preserving and adapting specialized craft techniques during a period of disrupted knowledge transmission.

Current Consensus and Continuing Debates

While scholarly perspectives on the Sea Peoples have diversified considerably, certain areas of consensus have emerged, while major areas of disagreement remain.

Recent archaeological discoveries continue to inform these debates. Excavations at Philistine sites like Ashkelon, Tell es-Safi/Gath, and Ekron have refined our understanding of Philistine material culture and settlement patterns (Maeir and Hitchcock 2017). Work at Hittite sites has clarified the nature of that empire's collapse (Singer 2000). Ongoing paleoclimate research provides increasingly precise data on environmental conditions. These accumulating findings promise to further refine our understanding of this pivotal historical episode.

New Perspectives and Emerging Evidence

The study of the Sea Peoples continues to evolve as new archaeological discoveries, analytical techniques, and theoretical approaches reshape our understanding of Late Bronze Age collapse. Several recent developments deserve particular attention for their potential to resolve longstanding questions or open new lines of inquiry.

Genetic Evidence and Population Movement

Perhaps the most significant recent development in Sea Peoples research has been the application of ancient DNA analysis to relevant archaeological contexts. In 2019, a groundbreaking study published in Science Advances analyzed DNA from 10 individuals excavated at the Philistine site of Ashkelon, comparing samples from the Late Bronze Age, early Iron Age, and later Iron Age periods (Feldman et al. 2019).

The results provided the first direct biological evidence for population movement associated with the Sea Peoples phenomenon. The study detected European-derived ancestry appearing in early Iron Age individuals (ca. 1200-1000 BCE) that was not present in earlier or later populations at the site. As the study's authors concluded: "These genetic results are compatible with a scenario in which the early Iron Age population of Ashkelon was formed by a mixture of local Levantine and foreign (likely Aegean-related) components" (Feldman et al. 2019: 9).

This genetic evidence supports the long-held archaeological interpretation of Philistine origins involving migration from the Aegean region, though it cannot specify the precise geographic source more narrowly. Intriguingly, the study also found that within approximately two centuries, this European genetic signature had been largely diluted through intermarriage with local populations—a pattern consistent with the gradual cultural assimilation visible in the archaeological record.

Similar genetic studies are now being conducted at other potential Sea Peoples sites, including locations in Cyprus, Anatolia, and the northern Levant. These investigations may help resolve debates about the geographic origins of different Sea Peoples groups and clarify patterns of population movement during the collapse period.

However, genetic evidence brings its own interpretive challenges. As archaeologist Philipp Stockhammer cautions: "Genetic data reveals biological ancestry, not cultural identity or language. We must be careful not to equate genetic profiles with ethnic groups or cultural formations, which involve complex social constructions beyond biological relatedness" (cited in Bachhuber 2021: 234).

Maritime Archaeology and Seaborne Movement

The maritime dimension of Sea Peoples activity has received renewed attention through underwater archaeology. Recent discoveries of shipwrecks dating to the Late Bronze Age collapse period offer potential insights into maritime technology, trade disruption, and naval warfare (Bass 1967; Pulak 1998).

The Cape Gelidonya and Uluburun shipwrecks off the coast of Turkey, though predating the main Sea Peoples period, provide important context for understanding Late Bronze Age maritime trade networks that were later disrupted. More directly relevant is the site at Point Iria near the Greek mainland, where a wreck dating to around 1200 BCE contained a mixed cargo of Cypriot, Cretan, and mainland Greek pottery—perhaps reflecting the kind of mixed maritime connections associated with Sea Peoples movements.

Maritime archaeologist Shelley Wachsmann has analyzed the distinctive Sea Peoples ships depicted in the Medinet Habu reliefs, identifying technical features that differentiate them from Egyptian vessels: "The Sea Peoples ships show clear Aegean features, including high angular stem and stern posts, bird-head devices, and distinctive arrangement of rowers. These vessels represent a maritime tradition separate from Egyptian shipbuilding practices" (Wachsmann 1998: 211).

Recent underwater surveys along Levantine, Cypriot, and Anatolian coastlines aim to locate harbor facilities and potential shipwrecks from this critical period. These investigations may eventually provide direct archaeological evidence for the maritime movements described in textual sources.

Reinterpreting Egyptian Sources

Egyptian depictions of conflict with the Sea Peoples, particularly the Medinet Habu reliefs commissioned by Ramesses III, have traditionally formed the cornerstone of Sea Peoples scholarship. Recent work has approached these sources with greater critical awareness of their propagandistic nature and artistic conventions (Roberts 2009).

Egyptologist Colleen Manassa's detailed analysis of the Medinet Habu naval battle scene reveals how Egyptian artistic conventions shaped the representation: "The battle is depicted according to established Egyptian iconographic principles for representing victory, with the pharaoh's overwhelming superiority emphasized through scale and positioning. This doesn't necessarily diminish the historical reality of the conflict, but requires us to read beyond the propagandistic elements" (cited in Ben-Dor Evian 2016: 165).

Similarly, translations of the accompanying texts have been refined. As Egyptologist Robert Ritner notes: "The Egyptian term previously translated as 'countries' or 'lands' in reference to the Sea Peoples might be better understood as 'tribal groups' or 'peoples,' without necessarily implying territorial states of origin" (cited in Kitchen 1996: 45).

These reinterpretations suggest a more nuanced understanding of Egyptian encounters with the Sea Peoples. Rather than a single massive invasion repelled in a decisive battle, the texts may describe a series of engagements with different groups over time, combined in the monument for ideological purposes. This reading aligns better with archaeological evidence for gradual rather than sudden changes in the region.

Systems Collapse Theory and Comparative Perspectives

The application of complex systems theory to the Bronze Age collapse has generated productive new frameworks for understanding the Sea Peoples phenomenon. This approach, developed by scholars like Eric Cline, A. Bernard Knapp, and Sturt Manning, views Late Bronze Age societies as interdependent networks where failures in one component could trigger cascading effects throughout the system (Knapp and Manning 2016).

As Cline argues in 1177 B.C.: "The Sea Peoples were as much the victims as the aggressors in the collapse... they both contributed to the perfect storm of calamities that brought down the Late Bronze Age and were swept up in the resulting tsunami of events" (Cline 2014: 173).

This systems perspective has been enriched by comparative studies examining other historical cases of complex society collapse, including the Maya, Western Roman Empire, and medieval Angkor (Middleton 2017). These comparisons reveal recurrent patterns in how complex societies respond to multiple concurrent stresses—particularly the tendency for interdependencies that provide advantages during stable periods to become vulnerabilities during crises.

Archaeologist Guy Middleton emphasizes the importance of human agency within these systemic processes: "Collapse is not simply something that happens to societies but involves choices made by individuals and groups responding to changing conditions. The Sea Peoples' movements represented one set of adaptive strategies among many possible responses to system stress" (Middleton 2017: 267).

This theoretical framework helps explain why the collapse affected different regions with varying intensity and why recovery followed diverse trajectories. It also accommodates the apparent heterogeneity of Sea Peoples groups while explaining their roughly contemporaneous movements as responses to similar systemic pressures.

Archaeological Evidence from New Regions

Excavations in previously under-studied regions have expanded our understanding of the geographic scope and varied manifestations of Bronze Age collapse and possible Sea Peoples activity.

In Anatolia, recent work at sites like Kinet Höyük and Kilise Tepe has documented destruction followed by cultural changes during the collapse period (Bachhuber 2021). At Tell Tayinat in southern Turkey, excavations have revealed a settlement with Aegean-style pottery and architecture dating to the early 12th century BCE, potentially representing Sea Peoples settlement outside the traditional Philistine heartland (Janeway 2006-2007).

On Cyprus, intensive investigation of sites like Enkomi, Kition, and Palaepaphos has clarified the island's complex experience during the collapse period—with some sites destroyed and abandoned, others showing continuity, and still others exhibiting evidence of new cultural elements potentially linked to Sea Peoples groups (Knapp 2013).

In the western Mediterranean, reassessment of sites in Sardinia, Sicily, and southern Italy has sought evidence for connections to Sea Peoples activity (Jung 2018). While direct archaeological confirmation of Sherden in Sardinia or Shekelesh in Sicily remains elusive, these investigations have documented significant cultural changes and disruptions in settlement patterns during the late 13th and 12th centuries BCE.

As archaeologist Christopher Monroe observes: "The expanded geographic scope of investigation has revealed the truly Mediterranean-wide nature of the transformations associated with Bronze Age collapse. The Sea Peoples were one manifestation of broader population movements and cultural changes affecting multiple regions simultaneously" (Monroe 2009: 187).

Chapter 9

POPULAR IMAGINATION AND FUTURE DIRECTIONS

Beyond academic research, the Sea Peoples have captured the popular imagination as symbols of mysterious, transformative historical change. Their association with civilizational collapse has made them recurring figures in both scholarly and public discourse about historical crisis and resilience.

The Sea Peoples in Historical Narratives

The Sea Peoples have featured prominently in broader historical narratives since their rediscovery in the 19th century. Early scholars like Gaston Maspero, who coined the term "Sea Peoples" in 1881, positioned them within frameworks of migration and invasion derived from contemporary European historical models (Breasted 1906). This approach often portrayed the Sea Peoples as an external force overwhelming established civilizations—a narrative that resonated with 19th century European concerns about barbarian invasions in classical history.

During the early-to-mid 20th century, archaeological discoveries at sites like Beth-Shean, Megiddo, and Ugarit seemed to provide material evidence for violent destruction associated with Sea Peoples invasions (Ussishkin 1985). Influential works like Claude Schaeffer's Stratigraphie Comparée et Chronologie de l'Asie Occidentale (1948) interpreted these destruction layers as evidence of coordinated, widespread catastrophe—a reading that aligned with the period's experience of world wars and societal upheaval (Schaeffer 1968).

By the late 20th century, more nuanced interpretations emerged. Scholars like Nancy Sandars emphasized the complex interplay between environmental factors, political instability, and population movements (Sandars 1985). The Sea Peoples were increasingly portrayed as both victims and agents of collapse rather than simply external destroyers. This shift reflected broader theoretical movements in archaeology away from invasion-based explanations toward multi-causal models incorporating environmental and socioeconomic factors.

In recent decades, the Sea Peoples have featured prominently in discussions of climate change impacts on historical societies. Books like Brian Fagan's The

Long Summer (2004) and Ronnie Ellenblum's The Collapse of the Eastern Mediterranean (2012) position the Bronze Age collapse as a case study in how climate stress can interact with political and economic vulnerabilities (cited in Kaniewski et al. 2013). This framing inevitably reflects contemporary concerns about climate change and societal resilience.

The Sea Peoples in Popular Culture

Beyond academic contexts, the Sea Peoples have appeared in various forms of popular culture, often serving as convenient historical mysteries or symbols of catastrophic change.

In fiction, they have featured in historical novels like Noel Gerson's The Raiders (1977) and David Gibbins' archaeological thriller Atlantis (2005), typically portrayed as fierce warriors bringing destruction to ancient civilizations. The mysterious aspects of their identity make them useful literary devices, allowing authors to project various characteristics onto them.

Documentary television has frequently covered the Sea Peoples, with programs like PBS's Secrets of the Dead: The Hittites and National Geographic's Ancient Apocalypse series featuring episodes on Bronze Age collapse. These presentations often emphasize the dramatic aspects of destruction and mystery, though recent productions have incorporated more nuanced scholarly perspectives on systems collapse.

Online discussions of the Sea Peoples reveal their enduring fascination for history enthusiasts. Internet forums, YouTube channels, and history podcasts regularly feature debates about their origins, impact, and relevance to understanding historical change. These discussions sometimes reflect outdated scholarly perspectives but demonstrate the topic's continuing resonance with public interest in historical mysteries and civilizational crisis.

Metaphorical Uses in Contemporary Discourse

Perhaps most interestingly, the Sea Peoples have become metaphorical figures in discussions of contemporary societal challenges. Journalists, academics, and commentators invoke them as shorthand for external threats to established systems or as symbols of how multiple stresses can overwhelm complex societies.

Environmental writers have drawn parallels between Bronze Age collapse and current climate challenges. In The Great Warming (2008), Brian Fagan explicitly connects the Sea Peoples phenomenon to contemporary climate migration: "Just as drought and changing climate patterns may have driven the Sea Peoples from their homes, climate change today creates environmental refugees who destabilize neighboring regions" (cited in Manning 2013: 485).

Political commentators across the ideological spectrum have appropriated the Sea Peoples as metaphors for contemporary migration and cultural change. Right-leaning writers sometimes invoke them when discussing modern immigration, while left-leaning commentators may use them to illustrate historical precedents for climate refugees or to critique simplistic "invasion" narratives.

Economic analysts have referenced Bronze Age collapse when discussing systemic risk in interconnected global systems. The Sea Peoples appear in discussions of how cascading failures can propagate through complex networks, with authors drawing parallels between Bronze Age trade disruption and potential vulnerabilities in modern supply chains.

As archaeologist Eric Cline reflects: "The continuing fascination with the Sea Peoples speaks to our enduring concerns about societal vulnerability and resilience. They serve as powerful symbols of how seemingly stable civilizations can experience rapid transformation through a combination of environmental stress, human movement, and systemic failures—concerns that resonate strongly in our own era of climate change, migration debates, and economic interconnection" (Cline 2014: 177).

Future Research

As research on the Sea Peoples continues to evolve, several promising directions and persistent questions define the current frontier of scholarship. These represent both opportunities for advancing our understanding and reminders of the inherent limitations in studying such a complex historical phenomenon with fragmentary evidence.

Methodological Innovations

Several emerging methodological approaches offer potential for resolving longstanding questions about the Sea Peoples:

Expanded Ancient DNA Analysis: Building on the groundbreaking Ashkelon study, researchers are applying ancient DNA analysis to human remains from other potential Sea Peoples contexts (Feldman et al. 2019). Projects underway at sites in Cyprus, the northern Levant, and Sardinia may help clarify population movements and relationships between different Sea Peoples groups.

Isotope Analysis: Strontium, oxygen, and lead isotope studies of human remains can identify non-local individuals by comparing isotope ratios in teeth and bones to local environmental baselines. Recent applications at Tiryns in Greece and Tell es-Safi/Gath in Israel have identified potential first-generation migrants, offering another line of evidence for population movement (Maeir et al. 2013).

Big Data Approaches: Computational analysis of large archaeological datasets is enabling more sophisticated modeling of collapse processes. Projects like the Modeling Ancient Settlement Systems (MASS) initiative are developing simulation models that can test different scenarios for how Bronze Age settlement systems responded to multiple stressors.

Remote Sensing and Geophysical Survey: Advanced remote sensing techniques are identifying previously unknown sites and features relevant to Bronze Age collapse. Satellite imagery analysis has revealed abandoned field systems potentially related to climate change, while marine geophysical surveys are locating submerged coastal sites and potential shipwrecks.

Scientific Dating Refinements: Improvements in radiocarbon dating precision, particularly through Bayesian modeling approaches, are enabling more fine-grained chronologies of collapse events (Manning 2013). This enhanced chronological resolution helps determine whether destructions were simultaneous or sequential—a crucial distinction for understanding collapse processes.

As archaeologist Sturt Manning notes: "The integration of these scientific approaches with traditional archaeological and textual analysis creates unprecedented opportunities for understanding the complex processes of Bronze Age collapse and the role of population movements within those processes" (Manning 2013: 492).

Persistent Questions and Challenges

Despite methodological advances, several fundamental questions about the Sea Peoples remain challenging to resolve:

The Question of Agency: To what extent were Sea Peoples movements coordinated or intentional versus reactive responses to circumstances? Did they possess unified leadership or political organization, or were they opportunistic aggregations of displaced groups? The nature of our evidence makes it difficult to access the decision-making processes and intentions behind their movements (Middleton 2017).

Identity Formation Processes: How did distinct Sea Peoples identities form and evolve during the collapse period? Were these pre-existing ethnic or cultural identities, or did they crystallize during the process of movement and conflict? The relationship between archaeological material culture and group identity remains theoretically complex (Yasur-Landau 2012).

Linguistic and Cultural Transmission: What languages did different Sea Peoples groups speak, and how did linguistic patterns shift during and after settlement? The limited textual evidence from this transitional period creates significant challenges for tracking linguistic change.

Scale and Demographics: How many people were involved in Sea Peoples movements, and what was their demographic composition? Archaeological evidence suggests family migration rather than purely military movement (Drews 2000), but quantifying the scale of population transfer remains difficult.

Alternative Narratives: How might our understanding change if we could access perspectives beyond the Egyptian accounts? The Sea Peoples' own understanding of their actions and identities remains inaccessible, forcing reliance on external descriptions filtered through Egyptian royal ideology (Ben-Dor Evian 2017).

As archaeologist Susan Sherratt observes: "These persistent questions remind us of the limitations inherent in studying past population movements through archaeological remains and texts produced by those who encountered them. The Sea Peoples will likely always retain some degree of mystery, not because they were inherently mysterious, but because of the fragmentary nature of our evidence for them" (Sherratt 1998: 313).

Theoretical Reorientations

Beyond specific methodological advances, several broader theoretical reorientations are reshaping Sea Peoples scholarship:

From Event to Process: Research increasingly frames the Sea Peoples phenomenon not as a discrete historical event but as a complex process unfolding over decades (Monroe 2009). This temporal extension allows for more nuanced understanding of how different factors interacted over time.

From Monocausal to Systems Thinking: Simplistic explanations attributing Bronze Age collapse primarily to Sea Peoples invasions or climate change have given way to systems models that examine how multiple factors interacted within complex networks of relationships (Knapp and Manning 2016).

From External Shock to Internal Vulnerability: Emphasis has shifted from viewing the Sea Peoples as an external shock to examining how internal vulnerabilities within Bronze Age societies conditioned their responses to various stressors, including population movements (Middleton 2017).

From Collapse to Transformation: Rather than focusing exclusively on destruction and discontinuity, scholarship increasingly examines how collapse processes created opportunities for new social, political, and cultural formations to emerge (Wengrow 2010).

From Centralized to Diverse Perspectives: Research is expanding beyond traditional focus on major centers to examine how collapse and transformation played out differently across diverse communities and regions (Bell 2006).

Archaeologist Aren Maeir suggests: "These theoretical shifts reflect broader changes in how we understand historical change—moving away from dramatic, event-based narratives toward recognition of complex processes involving multiple actors responding to changing conditions according to their particular circumstances and capabilities" (Maeir and Hitchcock 2017: 162).

Conclusion: The Enduring Significance of the Sea Peoples

The Sea Peoples phenomenon continues to fascinate scholars and the public alike not merely as a historical curiosity but as a compelling case study in how human societies respond to complex systemic challenges. Their story encapsulates fundamental questions about human adaptation, resilience, migration, cultural interaction, and societal transformation that remain relevant across historical contexts.

Beyond Simple Narratives

If this investigation has demonstrated anything, it is that simple narratives cannot capture the complexity of the Sea Peoples phenomenon. They were neither simply destructive invaders nor innocent refugees, neither the primary cause of Bronze Age collapse nor irrelevant to its processes (Cline 2014). They were diverse groups responding to changing conditions according to their capabilities and opportunities, sometimes accelerating systemic breakdown while simultaneously creating foundations for new cultural formations.

The evidence reviewed throughout this study reveals a mosaic of different trajectories: some Sea Peoples groups appear primarily as raiders and mercenaries, others as settlers establishing new communities, many likely transitioning between these roles as circumstances changed (Yasur-Landau 2010). Their impact varied dramatically by region—catastrophic in some areas, barely perceptible in others, and transformative but not destructive in still others.

This complexity should not be seen as an obstacle to understanding but rather as a more accurate reflection of how historical processes actually unfold. As archaeologist Shelley Wachsmann observes: "The very complexity that makes the Sea Peoples challenging to study also makes them valuable for understanding how human societies navigate periods of dramatic change" (Wachsmann 1998: 234).

Continuing Relevance

The Sea Peoples phenomenon offers valuable perspectives on several issues of continuing relevance:

Climate Resilience: The role of climate change in triggering and shaping Bronze Age collapse provides insights into how societies respond to environmental stress (Kaniewski et al. 2013). The varied outcomes across different regions—from complete collapse to successful adaptation—offer potential lessons for contemporary climate resilience planning.

Migration and Integration: The Philistine case demonstrates both the challenges and possibilities of population movement and cultural integration (Killebrew 2005). Their initial maintenance of distinctive cultural practices, followed by gradual integration with local populations while retaining certain traditions, illustrates processes still visible in modern migration contexts.

Systemic Risk: The cascading failures that characterized Bronze Age collapse highlight vulnerabilities created by interconnection and specialization—issues directly relevant to managing risk in our own highly interconnected global systems (Sherratt 2003).

Cultural Resilience and Innovation: The cultural innovations that emerged during and after collapse—from new writing systems to novel political arrangements—demonstrate how periods of disruption can create openings for significant innovation alongside undeniable hardship (Wengrow 2010).

Historical Contingency: The varied trajectories of different regions following collapse highlight how historical outcomes depend on specific combinations of circumstances rather than following predetermined patterns—a reminder that our own future remains open to multiple possibilities depending on how we respond to contemporary challenges.

The Future of Sea Peoples Research

As research continues, our understanding of the Sea Peoples will undoubtedly evolve further. New archaeological discoveries, advanced analytical techniques, and refined theoretical frameworks will resolve some existing questions while inevitably raising new ones (Oren 2000). The integration of archaeological evidence with paleoclimate data, textual analysis, and comparative historical studies promises increasingly sophisticated models of how the Late Bronze Age world transformed.

Yet certain aspects of the Sea Peoples phenomenon will likely remain elusive—their self-understanding, their specific motivations, the details of their movements before they entered the historical record. These limitations reflect the broader challenges of studying ancient population movements through archaeological remains and texts written by others.

Perhaps the most valuable contribution of continuing Sea Peoples research lies not in resolving all mysteries but in developing more sophisticated frameworks for understanding complex historical processes. By examining how multiple factors—environmental change, political structures, economic systems, technological developments, and human movement—interacted during this pivotal period, we gain insights applicable to other historical contexts and potentially to our own challenging times.

As we face our own era of climate change, population movement, political instability, and technological transformation, the study of how ancient societies navigated similar challenges offers valuable perspective. The Sea Peoples remind us that periods of dramatic change have occurred throughout human history, bringing both devastating disruption and opportunities for renewal and innovation. In their story, we may find insights for navigating our own uncertain future.

Final Reflections

The Sea Peoples will likely continue to fascinate both scholars and the public precisely because they embody fundamental questions about historical change: How do societies respond when faced with multiple concurrent challenges? What happens when established systems can no longer maintain themselves? How do people recreate their lives and communities when forced to leave their homes? How do different cultures interact and transform each other through contact, conflict, and coexistence?

These questions transcend their specific historical context to touch on enduring aspects of the human experience. As we continue to investigate the archaeological and textual traces left by these ancient peoples in movement, we gain not only knowledge of a particular historical episode but deeper insight into processes of societal transformation that remain relevant across time and place.

The Sea Peoples thus serve as powerful reminders that history is not simply a chronicle of steady progress or cyclical repetition, but a complex tapestry of adaptation, resilience, collapse, and renewal shaped by the interaction of environmental conditions, technological capabilities, social structures, and human choices (Broodbank 2013).

APPENDICES:

Chronology, Glossary, and Primary Texts

Chronology of the Late Bronze Age

To fully comprehend the complex sequence of events surrounding the Sea Peoples and the Bronze Age collapse, a detailed chronological framework is essential. The Late Bronze Age in the eastern Mediterranean spans approximately four centuries, with the most dramatic transformations occurring in its final century (Cline 2014). The following chronology highlights key events, archaeological contexts, and textual references that shape our understanding of this pivotal period:

1550-1400 BCE: Emergence of Late Bronze Age Systems

This period witnessed the consolidation of the major powers that would dominate the Late Bronze Age Mediterranean (Van De Mieroop 2016):

1550-1525 BCE: The expulsion of the Hyksos from Egypt and establishment of the 18th Dynasty, marking the beginning of Egypt's New Kingdom period (Shaw 2000). Pharaoh Ahmose I initiated Egyptian imperial expansion into the Levant.

1530-1500 BCE: Formation of the Mycenaean palace culture in mainland Greece, with increasing centralization of political and economic power (Dickinson 2006). Early shaft graves at Mycenae demonstrate growing elite wealth and connection to wider Mediterranean trade networks.

1520-1500 BCE: Consolidation of the Hittite Old Kingdom under Telepinu, establishing the foundations for later Hittite imperial expansion (Bryce 2005).

1500-1450 BCE: Expansion of Minoan influence throughout the Aegean, evidenced by the spread of Minoan artistic styles and administrative practices to islands including Thera, Rhodes, and Kythera.

1450 BCE: The Thera (Santorini) volcanic eruption, causing significant disruption across the eastern Mediterranean (Manning 2013). This event coincided with the decline of Minoan civilization and increased Mycenaean influence in the Aegean.

1425-1400 BCE: Establishment of the Mitanni Kingdom in northern Mesopotamia and Syria, creating a third major power alongside Egypt and the Hittites (Kuhrt 1995).

1400-1300 BCE: The Amarna Age and International System

This century represents the height of the Late Bronze Age international system, characterized by diplomatic correspondence, gift exchange, and formalized relations between "Great Kings" (Feldman 2006):

1390-1350 BCE: The Amarna period in Egypt under Amenhotep III and Akhenaten, documented through the Amarna Letters—diplomatic correspondence between Egypt and various Near Eastern kingdoms (Moran 1992).

1350-1330 BCE: Resurgence of Hittite power under Suppiluliuma I, who defeated Mitanni and established Hittite dominance in northern Syria (Bryce 2005).

1330-1300 BCE: First documented mentions of maritime raiders in Egyptian and Hittite texts. Pharaoh Seti I's inscriptions reference conflicts with the Sherden, while Hittite texts mention the Ahhiyawa (possibly Mycenaeans) causing trouble along the western Anatolian coast (Beckman, Bryce, and Cline 2011).

1315 BCE: Treaty between Ramesses II of Egypt and Hattusili III of Hatti, marking the stabilization of power relations following the Battle of Kadesh (1274 BCE) (Kitchen 1996).

1300-1250 BCE: Peak of international trade networks, evidenced by shipwrecks like Uluburun (c. 1300 BCE), carrying goods from at least seven different cultures (Bass et al. 1989).

1250-1200 BCE: Initial Signs of System Stress

This half-century shows increasing evidence of instability across multiple regions (Knapp and Manning 2016):

1250-1225 BCE: Destruction of several Mycenaean secondary centers, including Iolkos and Gla (Middleton 2010). These events mark the beginning of Mycenaean decline, though major palaces continued functioning.

1237 BCE: Tudhaliya IV of Hatti implements a trade embargo against Assyria, indicating growing economic competition and resource stress (Singer 2000).

1230-1220 BCE: Archaeological evidence of drought conditions begins to appear across the eastern Mediterranean, with paleoclimatic data showing decreased rainfall and agricultural productivity (Kaniewski et al. 2013).

1220-1210 BCE: First wave of destructions at Ugarit, Emar, and other Syrian sites, though these centers were subsequently rebuilt (Yon 1992).

1208 BCE: The Merneptah Stele records Egypt's victory over a coalition including Libyans and several Sea Peoples groups (Sherden, Shekelesh, Ekwesh, Lukka, and Teresh), marking the first major documented Sea Peoples incursion (Kitchen 1996).

1200 BCE: Destruction of Troy VIIa, potentially connected to regional instability and population movements (Cline 2009).

1200-1150 BCE: The Collapse Phase

This crucial half-century witnessed the most dramatic transformations across the eastern Mediterranean:

1197-1185 BCE: Comprehensive destruction of Mycenaean palace centers, including Mycenae, Tiryns, Pylos, and Thebes (Dickinson 2006). Linear B administrative systems cease functioning.

1190-1185 BCE: Final destruction of Hattusa, the Hittite capital, with evidence of abandonment rather than violent conquest (Bryce 2005). End of Hittite cuneiform records and imperial administration.

1185-1180 BCE: Destruction of Ugarit, documented in desperate letters describing enemy ships and approaching disaster (Pardee 2003). Cuneiform archives end abruptly, and the city is never reoccupied.

1180-1175 BCE: Ramesses III records the defeat of a major Sea Peoples coalition in his eighth regnal year, depicted on the walls of Medinet Habu (Kitchen 1996). The coalition includes the Peleset, Tjekker, Shekelesh, Denyen, and Weshesh.

1177-1175 BCE: Ramesses III records a second victory over Sea Peoples in his eleventh regnal year.

1175-1150 BCE: Initial establishment of Philistine settlements at Ashdod, Ashkelon, Ekron, Gath, and Gaza in the southern Levant, with distinctive Aegean-influenced material culture (Stager 1995).

1155-1150 BCE: End of the 20th Dynasty in Egypt and transition to the Third Intermediate Period, marking Egypt's decline as an imperial power (Shaw 2000).

1150-1050 BCE: Transition to the Early Iron Age

This century witnessed the consolidation of post-collapse political and cultural formations:

1150-1100 BCE: Emergence of Sub-Mycenaean pottery styles in Greece, marking cultural continuity despite political collapse (Dickinson 2006).

1130-1100 BCE: Formation of Neo-Hittite states in northern Syria and southeastern Anatolia, preserving elements of Hittite political ideology and artistic traditions (Hawkins 2000).

1100-1050 BCE: Development of distinctive Philistine material culture in the southern Levant, showing a mixture of Aegean and Levantine elements (Killebrew 2005).

1100-1050 BCE: Emergence of Phoenician city-states along the central Levantine coast, establishing the foundations for later Mediterranean colonization (Bell 2006).

1050-1000 BCE: Gradual transition to iron technology across the eastern Mediterranean, though the process occurred at different rates in different regions (Muhly 1985).

This chronological framework demonstrates that the Bronze Age collapse was neither sudden nor uniform (Middleton 2017). Rather, it represents a cascading series of failures across interconnected systems over approximately a century, with different regions experiencing disruption at different times and to varying degrees. The Sea Peoples movements occurred within this broader context of systemic transformation, serving as both symptoms and accelerants of collapse rather than its primary cause.

Glossary of Terms and Peoples

Major Cultures and Polities

Mycenaean Civilization: Late Bronze Age culture of mainland Greece (c. 1600-1100 BCE) centered around palace complexes that controlled regional economies through centralized administration documented on Linear B tablets (Kelder 2010). Major centers included Mycenae, Tiryns, Pylos, and Thebes.

Hittite Empire: Indo-European-speaking kingdom centered in central Anatolia (c. 1650-1180 BCE) that controlled much of Anatolia and northern Syria at its height (Bryce 2005). Ruled from the capital Hattusa, the empire was administered through a complex bureaucracy using cuneiform writing.

New Kingdom Egypt: Period of Egyptian history (c. 1550-1070 BCE) representing the height of Egyptian imperial power, with control extending from Nubia to the Euphrates River (Shaw 2000). The 19th and 20th Dynasties (Ramesside Period, c. 1292-1070 BCE) were contemporary with the Sea Peoples incursions.

Ugarit: Wealthy trading city on the northern Syrian coast, serving as a crucial nexus between Mesopotamian, Anatolian, and Mediterranean trade networks (Singer 1999). Destroyed c. 1185 BCE, its extensive archives provide vital information about the final years of the Bronze Age system.

Canaanite City-States: Network of small political entities in the southern Levant, often under Egyptian imperial control during the Late Bronze Age (Redford 1992). Major centers included Hazor, Megiddo, and Lachish.

Cypriote Polities: The island of Cyprus (Alashiya in ancient texts) hosted several small kingdoms during the Late Bronze Age, with economies heavily focused on copper production and maritime trade (Knapp 2013).

Minoan Civilization: Bronze Age culture of Crete (c. 2000-1450 BCE) characterized by palace complexes, distinctive artistic traditions, and the Linear A script. Though in decline by the Late Bronze Age collapse, Minoan cultural elements influenced Mycenaean civilization and wider Mediterranean cultures.

Sea Peoples Groups

Peleset/Philistines: The most extensively documented Sea Peoples group, who settled in the southern Levantine coastal plain following their defeat by Ramesses

III (Yasur-Landau 2010). Their material culture shows strong Aegean influences, and they are likely the same people mentioned in biblical texts as Philistines.

Sherden/Shardana: First mentioned in Egyptian texts during the Amarna period (14th century BCE), they initially appeared as raiders but later served as mercenaries in the Egyptian military (Emanuel 2013). Some scholars connect them with Sardinia, though this remains debated.

Shekelesh: Mentioned in both the Merneptah Stele and Ramesses III's inscriptions. Sometimes associated with Sicily (Sikels), though direct evidence remains limited (Vagnetti 2000).

Ekwesh: Mentioned in the Merneptah Stele as circumcised sea raiders allied with Libya. Some scholars identify them with the Ahhiyawa (Mycenaean Greeks) mentioned in Hittite texts (Beckman, Bryce, and Cline 2011).

Teresh: Sea raiders mentioned in both the Merneptah Stele and Ramesses III's inscriptions. Sometimes associated with the Tyrrhenians (Etruscans), though this identification remains speculative.

Tjekker: Sea Peoples group mentioned by Ramesses III who may have later settled in the central Levantine coast around Dor, based on the 11th century BCE Story of Wenamun (Wente 1990).

Denyen: Possibly connected to the Danuna mentioned in earlier Amarna letters and Hittite texts, and potentially related to the tribe of Dan in biblical sources or the Danaans mentioned by Homer (Singer 1999).

Weshesh: One of the less-documented Sea Peoples groups mentioned in Ramesses III's inscriptions. Their origins and fate remain obscure (Woudhuizen 2006).

Lukka: Maritime people from southwest Anatolia (classical Lycia) mentioned in Hittite, Egyptian, and Ugaritic texts as raiders and mercenaries (Singer 2000). They participated in the Battle of Kadesh against Egypt and are mentioned in the Amarna letters.

Archaeological Terms

Linear B: Syllabic script used to write Mycenaean Greek, primarily for administrative records (Davis 2008). Tablets document palace-centered economic systems that collapsed around 1200 BCE.

Bichrome Ware: Distinctive pottery style associated with early Philistine settlements, featuring red and black decoration on white slip, showing clear Aegean influences but produced locally in the Levant (Killebrew 1998).

Naue II Sword: Innovative slashing sword type that spread throughout the eastern Mediterranean during the Late Bronze Age collapse period, potentially associated with Sea Peoples warriors (Jung 2009).

Feathered Headdress: Distinctive headgear worn by certain Sea Peoples groups as depicted in Egyptian reliefs, particularly at Medinet Habu (Dothan 1982).

Hearth Room: Architectural feature found in early Philistine settlements, reflecting Aegean cultural practices transplanted to the Levant (Allen 1994).

Ashdoda Figurine: Distinctive Philistine female figurine type showing a seated woman with bird-like features, demonstrating the hybrid nature of early Philistine material culture (Dothan 1982).

Historical Concepts

Systems Collapse: Theoretical framework describing how interconnected complex systems can experience cascading failures when multiple stressors exceed adaptive capacity, resulting in rapid simplification and fragmentation (Middleton 2017).

Palace Economy: Centralized economic system characteristic of Late Bronze Age states, where royal institutions controlled production, storage, and distribution of goods through bureaucratic administration (Sherratt 2003).

Great Kings Correspondence: Diplomatic communication between rulers of major Late Bronze Age powers who recognized each other as equals, exemplified by the Amarna Letters and Hittite diplomatic archives (Moran 1992).

Dark Age: Period following the Bronze Age collapse characterized by reduced literacy, political fragmentation, and diminished archaeological visibility, particularly in Greece (c. 1100-800 BCE) (Dickinson 2006).

Orientalizing Period: Phase of increased Near Eastern influence on Greek culture following the Dark Age (c. 750-650 BCE), reflecting renewed Mediterranean connectivity.

Detailed Analysis of Key Primary Texts

The textual evidence for the Sea Peoples comes primarily from Egyptian and Ugaritic sources, with additional relevant material from Hittite archives. These texts provide crucial information about the identity, activities, and historical context of these groups, though they must be interpreted with attention to their political and cultural biases.

Egyptian Textual Sources

The Great Karnak Inscription of Merneptah (c. 1208 BCE)

This lengthy hieroglyphic text commemorates Pharaoh Merneptah's victory over a coalition of Libyans and Sea Peoples who attempted to invade Egypt from the west (Kitchen 1996). The inscription provides our first substantial mention of multiple Sea Peoples groups acting in concert:

"The wretched, fallen chief of Libya, Meryey son of Ded, has fallen upon the country of Tehenu with his bowmen... Sherden, Shekelesh, Ekwesh, Lukka, Teresh, taking the best of every warrior and every man of war of his country. He has brought his wife and his children... to the western boundary in the fields of Perire" (Breasted 1906, Vol. 3: 579).

This text reveals several crucial points: First, these early Sea Peoples groups operated in alliance with Libyan forces rather than as an independent coalition. Second, they are described as providing military specialists ("the best of every warrior") to the Libyan force, suggesting they may have served as mercenaries (Emanuel 2013). Third, the mention of wives and children indicates this was not merely a raiding party but a migration attempt.

The inscription continues with a detailed account of the battle, claiming that over 6,000 enemies were killed and providing specific numbers for each group. While these figures are likely exaggerated for propagandistic purposes, they suggest the Ekwesh constituted the largest contingent among the Sea Peoples groups.

A particularly intriguing detail concerns the Ekwesh, who are described as "foreskinless" or circumcised. Since circumcision was not generally practiced among Aegean populations, this detail has complicated efforts to identify the Ekwesh with Mycenaean Greeks (Ahhiyawa in Hittite texts), though some scholars suggest this may reflect Egyptian misunderstanding or propagandistic distortion.

The Medinet Habu Inscriptions of Ramesses III (c. 1180-1175 BCE)

The most extensive and detailed account of the Sea Peoples comes from Ramesses III's mortuary temple at Medinet Habu, which contains both relief carvings depicting battles against the Sea Peoples and accompanying hieroglyphic texts (Kitchen 1996). These materials document two separate conflicts: a naval battle in Ramesses' eighth regnal year and a land battle in his eleventh year.

The "Year 8" inscription describes a major coordinated invasion:

"The foreign countries made a conspiracy in their islands. All at once the lands were removed and scattered in the fray. No land could stand before their arms, from Hatti, Kode, Carchemish, Arzawa, and Alashiya on, being cut off at [one time]. A camp [was set up] in one place in Amurru. They desolated its people, and its land was like that which has never come into being. They were coming forward toward Egypt, while the flame was prepared before them. Their confederation was the Peleset, Tjekker, Shekelesh, Denyen, and Weshesh, lands united. They laid their hands upon the lands as far as the circuit of the earth, their hearts confident and trusting: 'Our plans will succeed!'" (Kitchen 1996: 18).

This text provides crucial information about the scope and nature of the Sea Peoples phenomenon. First, it describes a multi-regional collapse, with numerous states from Anatolia to Cyprus falling to the invaders before they turned toward Egypt. Second, it identifies five specific groups acting in confederation, a somewhat different roster than those mentioned in the earlier Merneptah inscription. Third, it characterizes the Sea Peoples as having originated in "islands," though this term could refer to coastal regions generally rather than literal islands.

The accompanying relief scenes provide valuable iconographic information about the Sea Peoples (Roberts 2009). They depict a naval battle in which Egyptian forces defeat a fleet of distinctive ships with bird-head prows, while Sea Peoples warriors are shown with characteristic features including feathered headdresses (Peleset), horned helmets (Sherden), and distinctive kilts and armor.

The "Year 11" inscription describes a subsequent conflict with the Sea Peoples allied with Libyan forces, suggesting that despite their earlier defeat, these groups remained active in the region:

"The northern countries quivered in their bodies, namely the Peleset and Tjekker. They cut off their soul and breathed [their last], for they had planned evil against Egypt. Their leaders were brought low through slaughter, for they came forward toward Egypt, [but] their advance was halted" (Kitchen 1996: 23).

This text indicates that even after their major defeat, certain Sea Peoples groups continued to threaten Egypt's interests, though apparently with diminished capacity. The inscription goes on to describe how captured Sea Peoples were incorporated into Egyptian military and labor systems:

"I settled them in strongholds, bound in my name. Their military classes were as numerous as hundred-thousands. I assigned portions for them all with clothing and provisions from the treasuries and granaries every year" (Kitchen 1996: 22).

This passage reveals an important aspect of Egyptian policy: rather than simply defeating the Sea Peoples, Egypt incorporated them into its imperial system, settling captured warriors in strategic locations as military colonists. This practice helps explain the archaeological evidence for Philistine settlements in the southern Levant, which appears to have occurred with Egyptian approval following the Philistines' defeat.

The Papyrus Harris I (c. 1150 BCE)

This lengthy papyrus, compiled shortly after Ramesses III's death, summarizes his accomplishments and donations to various temples (Breasted 1906). It includes a retrospective account of the Sea Peoples conflict:

"I extended all the boundaries of Egypt and overthrew those who had attacked them from their lands. I slew the Denyen in their islands, while the Tjekker and Peleset were made ashes. The Sherden and the Weshesh of the Sea were made non-existent, captured all together and brought in captivity to Egypt like the sands of the shore. I settled them in strongholds, bound in my name. Their military classes were as numerous as hundred-thousands" (Breasted 1906, Vol. 4: 403).

This account largely aligns with the Medinet Habu inscriptions but provides additional details about the fate of defeated Sea Peoples groups. The claim that some groups were "made ashes" or "made non-existent" contrasts with the statement that others were settled in Egypt, suggesting different groups received different treatment. The specific mention of defeating the Denyen "in their islands" provides rare information about the geographic origin of at least one Sea Peoples group.

Ugaritic Textual Sources

The coastal Syrian city of Ugarit, destroyed around 1185 BCE, has yielded several letters that document the final years before the Bronze Age collapse (Yon 1992). These texts provide a perspective on the Sea Peoples phenomenon from one of its victims rather than from Egypt, which successfully repelled them.

Letter of Ammurapi to the King of Alashiya (RS 18.147)

This dramatic letter from the last king of Ugarit to his counterpart in Cyprus expresses the desperate situation as enemy ships approached:

"My father, behold, the enemy ships came here; my cities were burned, and they did evil things in my country. Does not my father know that all my troops and chariots are in the Land of Hatti, and all my ships are in the Land of Lukka? They have not arrived here yet, and the country is thus left to itself... Consider this, my father, there are seven enemy ships that have come here and done evil things to me" (Pardee 2003: 101).

This text reveals several crucial points: First, Ugarit faced naval attacks by an unidentified enemy while its own military resources were deployed elsewhere, highlighting how the integrated Late Bronze Age system could create vulnerabilities when multiple crises occurred simultaneously. Second, the relatively small number of enemy ships (seven) suggests that even limited raids could threaten major centers when their defenses were compromised. Third, the letter demonstrates that communications between rulers continued to function even as the system was failing, with Ugarit seeking assistance from Cyprus.

Letter from an Ugaritic Official (RS 34.129)

Another letter from the final years of Ugarit describes the deteriorating security situation:

"When your messenger arrived, the army was humiliated and the city was sacked. Our food in the threshing floors was burnt and the vineyards were also destroyed. Our city is sacked. May you know it! May you know it!" (Schaeffer 1968: 87).

This vivid account describes the destruction of both the city and its agricultural resources, suggesting a comprehensive attack rather than a simple raid for portable wealth. The repeated phrase "May you know it!" conveys the writer's urgency and distress, providing a rare emotional perspective on the collapse events.

Letter Concerning Grain Shipments (RS 18.038)

Not all Ugaritic texts directly mention attacks, but some document the broader conditions of resource stress that accompanied the collapse:

"What have you done? You knew that there is famine in your house, but you did not seal and send the grain that was requested from you. Now, there is no grain in your house to keep us alive. So may you send us grain in ships quickly, to keep us alive!" (Singer 1999: 719).

This letter indicates that food shortages affected the region before Ugarit's final destruction, aligning with paleoclimatic evidence for drought conditions in the eastern Mediterranean during this period (Kaniewski et al. 2013). The text demonstrates how environmental stress compounded political and military challenges during the collapse phase.

Hittite Textual Sources

While Hittite texts do not directly describe the Sea Peoples by that name, they document increasing challenges along the empire's western frontiers in the decades before its collapse, providing context for understanding the broader regional instability (Singer 2000).

The Tawagalawa Letter (CTH 181)

This diplomatic letter from a Hittite king (likely Hattusili III) to the King of Ahhiyawa (likely a Mycenaean ruler) addresses conflicts in western Anatolia involving a renegade named Piyamaradu:

"Concerning the matter of Wilusa about which you wrote to me—saying that you were going to go to war, but now you have written to me [that you will not]... As for the fact that you wrote to me about making peace, it is good that we should do so. Let us not allow our subjects to commit acts of aggression against each other" (Beckman, Bryce, and Cline 2011: 101).

This text, dating to approximately 1250 BCE, documents tensions between the Hittite Empire and Mycenaean interests in western Anatolia several decades before the collapse. It suggests that diplomatic solutions were still possible at this stage, though the situation remained volatile.

The Šaušgamuwa Treaty (CTH 105)

This treaty between the Hittite king Tudhaliya IV and his vassal Šaušgamuwa of Amurru (c. 1230 BCE) includes provisions concerning maritime security:

"Ships of the land of Ahhiyawa must not go to him [the king of Assyria] from the land of Amurru. You must not allow his merchants to pass through your land, but do not hinder a ship of Assyria from reaching your land. Moreover, if a ship of the land of Ahhiyawa goes to the land of Assyria, you shall seize their crews and send them to my Majesty" (Hoffner 2009: 185).

This passage reveals increasing Hittite concerns about maritime security and trade control in the decades immediately preceding the collapse. The attempt to restrict Mycenaean (Ahhiyawan) shipping reflects growing tensions between major powers as the international system came under stress.

The Šuppiluliuma II Sea Battle Text (CTH 121)

This fragmentary text describes a naval battle conducted by the last documented Hittite king, Šuppiluliuma II (c. 1190-1180 BCE):

"The ships of the enemy came against me in three [groups]... I destroyed them, and I caught them and set fire to them in the sea" (Singer 2000: 24).

Though the identity of the enemy is not preserved, this rare description of a Hittite naval engagement shortly before the empire's collapse may document conflict with Sea Peoples groups. The text demonstrates that maritime threats had become significant enough to require direct military response from the Hittite king, representing a departure from earlier periods when the Hittite Empire focused primarily on land-based military operations.

Synthesis and Interpretation

When analyzed collectively, these primary texts reveal several key insights about the Sea Peoples and their role in the Bronze Age collapse:

Chronological Development: The texts document an escalating crisis, from initial raids mentioned in 14th-13th century sources to large-scale migrations and invasions in the early 12th century BCE. This progression suggests the Sea Peoples phenomenon intensified over time rather than appearing suddenly.

Diverse Identities: Different texts mention different combinations of groups under the Sea Peoples umbrella, indicating these were distinct populations rather than a single entity (Sherratt 1998). Some groups appear consistently across multiple sources (Sherden, Peleset), while others appear only in specific contexts.

Multiple Motivations: The texts suggest varied motivations among Sea Peoples groups, from raiding (early Sherden) to mercenary service (Sherden in Egyptian armies) to migration attempts (Peleset and others). This diversity cautions against simplistic characterizations of the Sea Peoples as merely pirates or invaders.

Systemic Context: Particularly in the Ugaritic and Hittite materials, we see evidence that Sea Peoples activities occurred within a broader context of systemic stress, including resource shortages, political tensions between established powers, and compromised defensive capabilities (Knapp and Manning 2016).

Aftermath Integration: Egyptian texts document how some defeated Sea Peoples groups were incorporated into new roles within surviving political systems, demonstrating that the collapse led to reorganization rather than simple destruction (Emanuel 2013).

These textual sources, while invaluable, present significant interpretive challenges. They primarily represent the perspective of established states confronting the Sea Peoples as external threats. We lack texts produced by the Sea Peoples themselves that might explain their own motivations, self-identity, or understanding of events. Additionally, the propagandistic nature of royal inscriptions like those of Ramesses III requires critical assessment of their claims (Ben-Dor Evian 2017).

When combined with archaeological evidence, however, these texts help construct a nuanced understanding of the Sea Peoples as both agents and products of the complex transformations that marked the end of the Bronze Age and the transition to new Iron Age political and cultural formations (Yasur-Landau 2010).

The Sea Peoples phenomenon thus emerges not as a simple historical event but as a multifaceted process in which diverse groups responded to and participated in systemic change. Their story reminds us that periods of dramatic transformation involve complex interactions between environmental conditions, political structures, economic systems, technological developments, and human agency—a lesson with continuing relevance as we navigate our own era of rapid change and global challenges (Cline 2014).

BIBLIOGRAPHY

Primary Sources

Cuneiform Texts and Translations

Albright, W.F. (1932). "The Syro-Mesopotamian God Sulman-Ešmun and Related Figures." *Archiv für Orientforschung* 7: 164-169.

Beckman, G. (1999). *Hittite Diplomatic Texts*. Second Edition. Atlanta: Scholars Press.

Beckman, G., Bryce, T., and Cline, E. (2011). *The Ahhiyawa Texts*. Atlanta: Society of Biblical Literature.

Breasted, J.H. (1906). *Ancient Records of Egypt: Historical Documents from the Earliest Times to the Persian Conquest*. 5 vols. Chicago: University of Chicago Press.

Edel, E. (1994). *Die ägyptisch-hethitische Korrespondenz aus Boghazköi in babylonischer und hethitischer Sprache*. 2 vols. Opladen: Westdeutscher Verlag.

Güterbock, H.G. (1992). "Survival of the Hittite Dynasty." In *The Crisis Years: The 12th Century B.C.*, edited by W.A. Ward and M.S. Joukowsky, 53-55. Dubuque: Kendall/Hunt.

Hawkins, J.D. (2000). *Corpus of Hieroglyphic Luwian Inscriptions. Volume I: Inscriptions of the Iron Age*. Berlin: De Gruyter.

Hoffner, H.A. (2009). *Letters from the Hittite Kingdom*. Atlanta: Society of Biblical Literature.

Kitchen, K.A. (1996). *Ramesside Inscriptions Translated and Annotated: Notes and Comments*. Vol. 2. Oxford: Blackwell.

Moran, W.L. (1992). *The Amarna Letters*. Baltimore: Johns Hopkins University Press.

Otten, H. (1963). "Neue Quellen zum Ausklang des Hethitischen Reiches." *Mitteilungen der Deutschen Orient-Gesellschaft* 94: 1-23.

Pardee, D. (2003). "The Ugaritic Texts." In *The Context of Scripture*, edited by W.W. Hallo and K.L. Younger, Vol. 1, 87-114. Leiden: Brill.

Singer, I. (2000). "New Evidence on the End of the Hittite Empire." In *The Sea Peoples and Their World: A Reassessment*, edited by E.D. Oren, 21-33. Philadelphia: University of Pennsylvania Museum.

Wente, E.F. (1990). *Letters from Ancient Egypt*. Atlanta: Scholars Press.

Archaeological Reports

Artzy, M. (2013). "On the Other 'Sea Peoples'." In *The Philistines and Other 'Sea Peoples' in Text and Archaeology*, edited by A.E. Killebrew and G. Lehmann, 329-344. Atlanta: Society of Biblical Literature.

Bass, G.F. (1967). *Cape Gelidonya: A Bronze Age Shipwreck*. Transactions of the American Philosophical Society 57.8. Philadelphia: American Philosophical Society.

Bass, G.F., Pulak, C., Collon, D., and Weinstein, J. (1989). "The Bronze Age Shipwreck at Ulu Burun: 1986 Campaign." *American Journal of Archaeology* 93(1): 1-29.

Ben-Dor Evian, S. (2017). "Ramesses III and the 'Sea-Peoples': Towards a New Philistine Paradigm." *Oxford Journal of Archaeology* 36(3): 267-285.

Betancourt, P.P. (2000). "The Aegean and the Origin of the Sea Peoples." In *The Sea Peoples and Their World: A Reassessment*, edited by E.D. Oren, 297-303. Philadelphia: University of Pennsylvania Museum.

Dothan, T. (1982). *The Philistines and Their Material Culture*. New Haven: Yale University Press.

Dothan, T., and Dothan, M. (1992). *People of the Sea: The Search for the Philistines*. New York: Macmillan.

Finkelstein, I. (1995). "The Philistine Countryside." *Israel Exploration Journal* 45(4): 224-242.

Gjerstad, E. (1944). "The Colonization of Cyprus in Greek Legend." *Opuscula Archaeologica* 3: 107-123.

Karageorghis, V. (1992). "The Crisis Years: Cyprus." In *The Crisis Years: The 12th Century B.C.*, edited by W.A. Ward and M.S. Joukowsky, 79-86. Dubuque: Kendall/Hunt.

Killebrew, A.E. (2005). *Biblical Peoples and Ethnicity: An Archaeological Study of Egyptians, Canaanites, Philistines, and Early Israel, 1300-1100 B.C.E.* Atlanta: Society of Biblical Literature.

Lehmann, G. (2013). "Aegean-Style Pottery in Syria and Lebanon during Iron Age I." In *The Philistines and Other 'Sea Peoples' in Text and Archaeology*, edited by A.E. Killebrew and G. Lehmann, 265-328. Atlanta: Society of Biblical Literature.

Maeir, A.M., Hitchcock, L.A., and Horwitz, L.K. (2013). "On the Constitution and Transformation of Philistine Identity." *Oxford Journal of Archaeology* 32(1): 1-38.

Mountjoy, P.A. (2013). "The Mycenaean IIIC Pottery at Tell Kazel, Syria." In *The Philistines and Other 'Sea Peoples' in Text and Archaeology*, edited by A.E. Killebrew and G. Lehmann, 349-370. Atlanta: Society of Biblical Literature.

Pulak, C. (1998). "The Uluburun Shipwreck: An Overview." *International Journal of Nautical Archaeology* 27(3): 188-224.

Schaeffer, C.F.A. (1968). *Ugaritica V: Nouveaux textes accadiens, hourrites et ugaritiques des archives et bibliothèques privées d'Ugarit.* Paris: Geuthner.

Stager, L.E. (1995). "The Impact of the Sea Peoples in Canaan (1185-1050 BCE)." In *The Archaeology of Society in the Holy Land*, edited by T.E. Levy, 332-348. London: Leicester University Press.

Ussishkin, D. (1985). "Levels VII and VI at Tel Lachish and the End of the Late Bronze Age in Canaan." In *Palestine in the Bronze and Iron Ages: Papers in Honour of Olga Tufnell*, edited by J.N. Tubb, 213-230. London: Institute of Archaeology.

Yasur-Landau, A. (2010). *The Philistines and Aegean Migration at the End of the Late Bronze Age*. Cambridge: Cambridge University Press.

Yon, M. (1992). "The End of the Kingdom of Ugarit." In *The Crisis Years: The 12th Century B.C.*, edited by W.A. Ward and M.S. Joukowsky, 111-122. Dubuque: Kendall/Hunt.

Secondary Scholarship

Monographs

Adams, M.J., and Cohen, M.E. (2013). *The "Sea Peoples" in Primary Sources.* In *The Philistines and Other "Sea Peoples" in Text and Archaeology*, edited by A.E. Killebrew and G. Lehmann, 645-664. Atlanta: Society of Biblical Literature.

Bachhuber, C. (2021). *Seafaring and Mobility in the Late Bronze Age Eastern Mediterranean.* Cambridge: Cambridge University Press.

Barako, T.J. (2013). *Philistines and Egyptians in Southern Coastal Canaan During the Early Iron Age.* In *The Philistines and Other "Sea Peoples" in Text and Archaeology*, edited by A.E. Killebrew and G. Lehmann, 37-51. Atlanta: Society of Biblical Literature.

Broodbank, C. (2013). *The Making of the Middle Sea: A History of the Mediterranean from the Beginning to the Emergence of the Classical World.* London: Thames & Hudson.

Bryce, T. (2005). *The Kingdom of the Hittites.* New Edition. Oxford: Oxford University Press.

Cline, E.H. (2014). *1177 B.C.: The Year Civilization Collapsed.* Princeton: Princeton University Press.

Davis, J.L. (2008). *Mycenaean Pottery.* In *The Archaeology of Greece and Rome: Studies in Honour of Anthony Snodgrass*, edited by J.L. Bintliff and K.A. Sbonias, 29-57. Edinburgh: Edinburgh University Press.

Dickinson, O. (2006). *The Aegean from Bronze Age to Iron Age: Continuity and Change Between the Twelfth and Eighth Centuries BC.* London: Routledge.

Drews, R. (1993). *The End of the Bronze Age: Changes in Warfare and the Catastrophe ca. 1200 B.C.* Princeton: Princeton University Press.

Finkelstein, I. (2002). *The Philistines in the Bible: A Late-Monarchic Perspective. Journal for the Study of the Old Testament* 27(2): 131-167.

Fischer, P.M. (2014). *The Southern Levant (Transjordan) During the Late Bronze Age.* In *The Oxford Handbook of the Archaeology of the Levant: c. 8000-332 BCE*, edited by M.L. Steiner and A.E. Killebrew, 561-576. Oxford: Oxford University Press.

Gilboa, A. (2005). *Sea Peoples and Phoenicians along the Southern Phoenician Coast—A Reconciliation: An Interpretation of Šikila (SKL) Material Culture. Bulletin of the American Schools of Oriental Research* 337: 47-78.

Hitchcock, L.A., and Maeir, A.M. (2014). *Yo-ho, yo-ho, a Seren's Life for Me! World Archaeology* 46(4): 624-640.

Janeway, B. (2017). *Sea Peoples of the Northern Levant? Aegean-Style Pottery from Early Iron Age Tell Tayinat.* Winona Lake: Eisenbrauns.

Jung, R. (2009). *Pirates of the Aegean: Italy – East Aegean – Cyprus at the End of the Second Millennium BCE.* In *Cyprus and the East Aegean: Intercultural*

Contacts from 3000 to 500 BC, edited by V. Karageorghis and O. Kouka, 72-93. Nicosia: A.G. Leventis Foundation.

Kelder, J.M. (2010). *The Kingdom of Mycenae: A Great Kingdom in the Late Bronze Age Aegean*. Bethesda: CDL Press.

Killebrew, A.E., and Lehmann, G., eds. (2013). *The Philistines and Other "Sea Peoples" in Text and Archaeology*. Atlanta: Society of Biblical Literature.

Knapp, A.B., and Manning, S.W. (2016). *Crisis in Context: The End of the Late Bronze Age in the Eastern Mediterranean*. American Journal of Archaeology 120(1): 99-149.

Kuhrt, A. (1995). *The Ancient Near East c. 3000-330 BC*. 2 vols. London: Routledge.

Middleton, G.D. (2017). *Understanding Collapse: Ancient History and Modern Myths*. Cambridge: Cambridge University Press.

Molloy, B. (2016). *Nought May Endure but Mutability: Eclectic Encounters and Material Change in the 13th to 11th Centuries BC Aegean*. In *Of Odysseys and Oddities: Scales and Modes of Interaction Between Prehistoric Aegean Societies and Their Neighbours*, edited by B. Molloy, 343-384. Oxford: Oxbow.

Morkot, R. (2013). *From Conquered to Conqueror: The Organization of Nubia in the New Kingdom and the Kushite Administration of Egypt*. In *Ancient Egyptian Administration*, edited by J.C. Moreno García, 911-963. Leiden: Brill.

Mumford, G. (2014). *Egypt and the Levant*. In *The Oxford Handbook of the Archaeology of the Levant: c. 8000-332 BCE*, edited by M.L. Steiner and A.E. Killebrew, 69-89. Oxford: Oxford University Press.

Oren, E.D., ed. (2000). *The Sea Peoples and Their World: A Reassessment*. Philadelphia: University of Pennsylvania Museum.

Redford, D.B. (1992). *Egypt, Canaan, and Israel in Ancient Times*. Princeton: Princeton University Press.

Roberts, R.G. (2009). *Identity, Choice, and the Year 8 Reliefs of Ramesses III at Medinet Habu*. In *Forces of Transformation: The End of the Bronze Age in the Mediterranean*, edited by C. Bachhuber and R.G. Roberts, 60-68. Oxford: Oxbow.

Routledge, B., and McGeough, K. (2009). *Just What Collapsed? A Network Perspective on "Palatial" and "Private" Trade at Ugarit.* In *Forces of Transformation: The End of the Bronze Age in the Mediterranean*, edited by C. Bachhuber and R.G. Roberts, 22-29. Oxford: Oxbow.

Sandars, N.K. (1985). *The Sea Peoples: Warriors of the Ancient Mediterranean*. Revised Edition. London: Thames & Hudson.

Shaw, I., ed. (2000). *The Oxford History of Ancient Egypt*. Oxford: Oxford University Press.

Sherratt, S. (1998). *"Sea Peoples" and the Economic Structure of the Late Second Millennium in the Eastern Mediterranean.* In *Mediterranean Peoples in Transition: Thirteenth to Early Tenth Centuries BCE*, edited by S. Gitin, A. Mazar, and E. Stern, 292-313. Jerusalem: Israel Exploration Society.

Sherratt, S. (2003). *The Mediterranean Economy: "Globalization" at the End of the Second Millennium B.C.E.* In *Symbiosis, Symbolism, and the Power of the Past: Canaan, Ancient Israel, and Their Neighbors from the Late Bronze Age through Roman Palaestina*, edited by W.G. Dever and S. Gitin, 37-62. Winona Lake: Eisenbrauns.

Singer, I. (2017). *The Philistines in the North and the Kingdom of Taita.* In *The Late Bronze and Early Iron Ages of Southern Canaan*, edited by S. Gitin, A. Maeir, and J. Uziel, 149-156. Berlin: De Gruyter.

Stern, E. (2013). *The Material Culture of the Northern Sea Peoples in Israel*. Winona Lake: Eisenbrauns.

Tubb, J.N. (2000). *Sea Peoples in the Jordan Valley.* In *The Sea Peoples and Their World: A Reassessment*, edited by E.D. Oren, 181-196. Philadelphia: University of Pennsylvania Museum.

Van De Mieroop, M. (2016). *A History of the Ancient Near East ca. 3000-323 BC*. Third Edition. Oxford: Wiley-Blackwell.

Ward, W.A., and Joukowsky, M.S., eds. (1992). *The Crisis Years: The 12th Century B.C. From Beyond the Danube to the Tigris*. Dubuque: Kendall/Hunt.

Weeden, M. (2013). *After the Hittites: The Kingdoms of Karkamish and Palistin in Northern Syria*. Bulletin of the Institute of Classical Studies 56(2): 1-20.

Woudhuizen, F.C. (2006). *The Ethnicity of the Sea Peoples*. Rotterdam: Erasmus University.

Yasur-Landau, A. (2012). *The Role of the Canaanite Population in the Aegean Migration to the Southern Levant in the Late Second Millennium BCE*. In *Materiality and Social Practice: Transformative Capacities of Intercultural Encounters*, edited by J. Maran and P.W. Stockhammer, 191-197. Oxford: Oxbow.

Articles and Dissertations

Allen, S.H. (1994). "Trojan Grey Ware at Tel Miqne-Ekron." *Bulletin of the American Schools of Oriental Research* 293: 39-51.

Artzy, M. (1997). "Nomads of the Sea." In *Res Maritimae: Cyprus and the Eastern Mediterranean from Prehistory to Late Antiquity*, edited by S. Swiny, R.L. Hohlfelder, and H.W. Swiny, 1-16. Atlanta: Scholars Press.

Bachhuber, C. (2006). "Aegean Interest on the Uluburun Ship." *American Journal of Archaeology* 110(3): 345-363.

Barako, T.J. (2000). "The Philistine Settlement as Mercantile Phenomenon?" *American Journal of Archaeology* 104(3): 513-530.

Bauer, A.A. (1998). "Cities of the Sea: Maritime Trade and the Origin of Philistine Settlement in the Early Iron Age Southern Levant." *Oxford Journal of Archaeology* 17(2): 149-168.

Bell, C. (2006). *The Evolution of Long Distance Trading Relationships across the LBA/Iron Age Transition on the Northern Levantine Coast: Crisis, Continuity and Change*. Oxford: Archaeopress.

Ben-Dor Evian, S. (2016). "The Battles between Ramesses III and the 'Sea-Peoples': When, Where and Who? An Iconic Analysis of the Egyptian Reliefs." *Zeitschrift für Ägyptische Sprache und Altertumskunde* 143(2): 151-168.

Bryce, T. (2016). "The Land of Hiyawa (Que) Revisited." *Anatolian Studies* 66: 67-79.

Burke, A.A. (2008). "'Walled Up to Heaven': The Evolution of Middle Bronze Age Fortification Strategies in the Levant." *Studies in the Archaeology and History of the Levant* 4. Winona Lake: Eisenbrauns.

Cline, E.H. (2009). "Achilles in Anatolia: Myth, History, and the Aššuwa Rebellion." In *Quaestiones Praehistoricae: Studia in honorem Marie-Henriette et Valentin Dédéyan*, edited by A. Anastassiou and D. Panagopoulou, 357-365. Louvain-la-Neuve: Peeters.

Cline, E.H., and O'Connor, D. (2003). "The Mystery of the 'Sea Peoples'." In *Mysterious Lands*, edited by D. O'Connor and S. Quirke, 107-138. London: UCL Press.

Davis, D. (2011). "The Problem of the Origin of Greek Sacrifice: The Minoan-Mycenaean Evidence." Ph.D. dissertation, University of Melbourne.

Dietrich, M., and Loretz, O. (2002). "Der Untergang von Ugarit am 21. Januar 1192 v. Chr.? Der astronomisch-hepatoskopische Bericht KTU 1.78 (RS 12.061)." *Ugarit-Forschungen* 34: 53-74.

Drews, R. (2000). "Medinet Habu: Oxcarts, Ships, and Migration Theories." *Journal of Near Eastern Studies* 59(3): 161-190.

Emanuel, J.P. (2013). "Šrdn from the Sea: The Arrival, Integration, and Acculturation of a 'Sea People'." *Journal of Ancient Egyptian Interconnections* 5(1): 14-27.

Feldman, M.H. (2006). *Diplomacy by Design: Luxury Arts and an "International Style" in the Ancient Near East, 1400-1200 BCE*. Chicago: University of Chicago Press.

Finkelstein, I. (2000). "The Philistine Settlements: When, Where and How Many?" In *The Sea Peoples and Their World: A Reassessment*, edited by E.D. Oren, 159-180. Philadelphia: University of Pennsylvania Museum.

Fischer, P.M. (2007). "A New Perspective on the Sea Peoples Phenomenon." In *The Synchronisation of Civilisations in the Eastern Mediterranean in the Second Millennium B.C. III*, edited by M. Bietak and E. Czerny, 251-265. Vienna: Österreichische Akademie der Wissenschaften.

Gilboa, A., Sharon, I., and Boaretto, E. (2008). "Tel Dor and the Chronology of Phoenician 'Pre-Colonization' Stages." In *Beyond the Homeland: Markers in Phoenician Chronology*, edited by C. Sagona, 113-204. Leuven: Peeters.

Gitin, S., Mazar, A., and Stern, E., eds. (1998). *Mediterranean Peoples in Transition: Thirteenth to Early Tenth Centuries BCE*. Jerusalem: Israel Exploration Society.

Goren, Y., Finkelstein, I., and Na'aman, N. (2004). *Inscribed in Clay: Provenance Study of the Amarna Tablets and Other Ancient Near Eastern Texts*. Tel Aviv: Emery and Claire Yass Publications in Archaeology.

Hitchcock, L.A., and Maeir, A.M. (2016). "A Pirate's Life for Me: The Maritime Culture of the Sea Peoples." *Palestine Exploration Quarterly* 148(4): 245-264.

Janeway, B. (2006-2007). "The Nature and Extent of Aegean Contact at Tell Ta'yinat and Vicinity in the Early Iron Age: Evidence of the Sea Peoples?" *Scripta Mediterranea* 27-28: 123-146.

Jung, R. (2018). "Push and Pull Factors of the Sea Peoples between Italy and the Levant." In *The Late Bronze Age in the Aegean*, edited by J. Driessen, 273-306. Louvain-la-Neuve: Presses Universitaires de Louvain.

Kaniewski, D., et al. (2010). "Late Second-Early First Millennium BC Abrupt Climate Changes in Coastal Syria and Their Possible Significance for the History of the Eastern Mediterranean." *Quaternary Research* 74(2): 207-215.

Kaniewski, D., et al. (2013). "Environmental Roots of the Late Bronze Age Crisis." *PLoS ONE* 8(8): e71004.

Killebrew, A.E. (1998). "Ceramic Typology and Technology of Late Bronze II and Iron I Assemblages from Tel Miqne-Ekron: The Transition from Canaanite to Philistine Culture." In *Mediterranean Peoples in Transition*, edited by S. Gitin, A. Mazar, and E. Stern, 379-405. Jerusalem: Israel Exploration Society.

Knapp, A.B. (2013). *The Archaeology of Cyprus: From Earliest Prehistory through the Bronze Age*. Cambridge: Cambridge University Press.

Kopanias, K. (2017). "The Sea Peoples at Hala Sultan Tekke, Cyprus: Fact or Fiction?" *Journal of Eastern Mediterranean Archaeology and Heritage Studies* 5(3-4): 137-146.

Kuhrt, A. (2002). "Greek Contact with the Levant and Mesopotamia in the First Half of the First Millennium BC: A View from the East." In *Greek Settlements in the Eastern Mediterranean and the Black Sea*, edited by G.R. Tsetskhladze and A.M. Snodgrass, 17-25. Oxford: Archaeopress.

Maeir, A.M., and Hitchcock, L.A. (2017). "The Appearance, Formation and Transformation of Philistine Culture: New Perspectives and New Finds." In *The Sea Peoples Up-To-Date: New Research on Transformations in the Eastern Mediterranean in the 13th-11th Centuries BCE*, edited by P.M. Fischer and T. Bürge, 149-162. Vienna: Austrian Academy of Sciences Press.

Manning, S.W. (2013). "The Roman World and Climate: Context, Text, and Pretexts." *Journal of Roman Archaeology* 26: 465-492.

Maran, J. (2009). "The Crisis Years? Reflections on Signs of Instability in the Last Decades of the Mycenaean Palaces." *Scienze dell'Antichità* 15: 241-262.

Master, D.M. (2001). "State Formation Theory and the Kingdom of Ancient Israel." *Journal of Near Eastern Studies* 60(2): 117-131.

Middleton, G.D. (2010). "The Collapse of Palatial Society in LBA Greece and the Postpalatial Period." Ph.D. dissertation, Durham University.

Monroe, C.M. (2009). *Scales of Fate: Trade, Tradition, and Transformation in the Eastern Mediterranean ca. 1350-1175 BCE*. Münster: Ugarit-Verlag.

Mountjoy, P.A. (1998). "The East Aegean-West Anatolian Interface in the Late Bronze Age: Mycenaeans and the Kingdom of Ahhiyawa." *Anatolian Studies* 48: 33-67.

Nur, A., and Cline, E.H. (2000). "Poseidon's Horses: Plate Tectonics and Earthquake Storms in the Late Bronze Age Aegean and Eastern Mediterranean." *Journal of Archaeological Science* 27(1): 43-63.

Pedrazzi, T. (2013). "The Sea Peoples in the Levant: A North Syrian Perspective." In *The Philistines and Other "Sea Peoples" in Text and Archaeology*, edited by A.E. Killebrew and G. Lehmann, 439-471. Atlanta: Society of Biblical Literature.

Pritchard, J.B. (1969). *Ancient Near Eastern Texts Relating to the Old Testament*. Third Edition with Supplement. Princeton: Princeton University Press.

Pulak, C. (2008). "The Uluburun Shipwreck and Late Bronze Age Trade." In *Beyond Babylon: Art, Trade, and Diplomacy in the Second Millennium B.C.*, edited by J. Aruz, K. Benzel, and J.M. Evans, 289-310. New Haven: Yale University Press.

Roberts, R.G. (2008). "Identity, Choice, and the Year 8 Reliefs of Ramesses III at Medinet Habu." In *Forces of Transformation: The End of the Bronze Age in the Mediterranean*, edited by C. Bachhuber and R.G. Roberts, 60-68. Oxford: Oxbow.

Sherratt, S. (2013). "The Ceramic Phenomenon of the 'Sea Peoples': An Overview." In *The Philistines and Other "Sea Peoples" in Text and Archaeology*, edited by A.E. Killebrew and G. Lehmann, 619-644. Atlanta: Society of Biblical Literature.

Singer, I. (1999). "A Political History of Ugarit." In *Handbook of Ugaritic Studies*, edited by W.G.E. Watson and N. Wyatt, 603-733. Leiden: Brill.

Stager, L.E. (1991). "When Canaanites and Philistines Ruled Ashkelon." *Biblical Archaeology Review* 17(2): 24-43.

Stern, E. (2000). "The Settlement of Sea Peoples in Northern Israel." In *The Sea Peoples and Their World: A Reassessment*, edited by E.D. Oren, 197-212. Philadelphia: University of Pennsylvania Museum.

Vagnetti, L. (2000). "Western Mediterranean Overview: Peninsular Italy, Sicily and Sardinia at the Time of the Sea Peoples." In *The Sea Peoples and Their World: A Reassessment*, edited by E.D. Oren, 305-326. Philadelphia: University of Pennsylvania Museum.

Weeden, M. (2013). "After the Hittites: The Kingdoms of Karkamish and Palistin in Northern Syria." *Bulletin of the Institute of Classical Studies* 56(2): 1-20.

Weinstein, J.M. (1992). "The Collapse of the Egyptian Empire in the Southern Levant." In *The Crisis Years: The 12th Century B.C.*, edited by W.A. Ward and M.S. Joukowsky, 142-150. Dubuque: Kendall/Hunt.

Wengrow, D. (2010). *What Makes Civilization? The Ancient Near East and the Future of the West*. Oxford: Oxford University Press.

Yasur-Landau, A. (2003). "Why Can't We Find the Origin of the Philistines? In Search of the Source of a Peripheral Aegean Culture." *Near Eastern Archaeology* 66(1-2): 30-32.

Zuckerman, S. (2007). "Anatomy of a Destruction: Crisis Architecture, Termination Rituals and the Fall of Canaanite Hazor." *Journal of Mediterranean Archaeology* 20(1): 3-32.

Digital Resources and Online Databases

American Schools of Oriental Research (ASOR). (2020). *The Ancient Near East Today*. http://www.asor.org/anetoday/

Archi, A., et al. (2019). *Hethitologie Portal Mainz*. https://www.hethport.uni-wuerzburg.de/

British Museum. (2021). *Collection Online*. https://www.britishmuseum.org/collection

Cuneiform Digital Library Initiative (CDLI). (2021). https://cdli.ucla.edu/

Digital Egypt for Universities. (2018). University College London. https://www.ucl.ac.uk/museums-static/digitalegypt/

Digital Karnak. (2019). University of California, Los Angeles. http://dlib.etc.ucla.edu/projects/Karnak/

Electronic Text Corpus of Sumerian Literature. (2021). University of Oxford. http://etcsl.orinst.ox.ac.uk/

Louvre Museum. (2021). *Atlas Database of Exhibits*. https://collections.louvre.fr/en/

Metropolitan Museum of Art. (2021). *Collection Database*. https://www.metmuseum.org/art/collection

Oriental Institute of the University of Chicago. (2021). *Abzu: Guide to Resources for the Study of the Ancient Near East*. https://www.etana.org/abzu

Oxford Ashmolean Museum. (2021). *Eastern Art Online*. https://jameelcentre.ashmolean.org/

Penn Museum. (2021). *Digital Collections*. https://www.penn.museum/collections/

Tell es-Safi/Gath Archaeological Project. (2021). Bar-Ilan University. https://gath.wordpress.com/

COMING SOON...

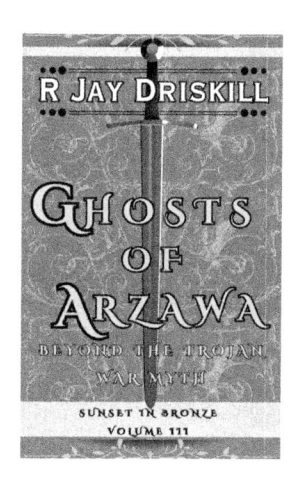

Sunset in Bronze volume III

Ghosts of Arzawa: Beyond the Trojan War Myth

Unearth Arzawa, the forgotten Bronze Age power of Western Anatolia!

This book reveals a formidable kingdom that defied the Hittites and influenced the Trojan War myths. Explore its culture, geopolitics, and figures like Piyama-radu through archaeological finds and re-evaluated texts.

A compelling new perspective on a pivotal lost civilization.

ABOUT THE AUTHOR

R Jay Driskill is an archaeologist and an ardent explorer of history's deepest mysteries, bringing ancient worlds to life through compelling non-fiction and fiction. With a background rooted at the University of Florida, Driskill meticulously researches each story, blending scholarly insight with thrilling narratives that transport readers across millennia.

Whether you're fascinated by ancient civilizations, historical fiction, or thrilling archaeological mysteries, R Jay Driskill offers meticulously crafted stories that entertain, educate, and keep you turning pages late into the night.

Explore his books today and embark on an adventure through time!

Read more at rjaydriskill.com

If you enjoyed *Raiders of the Bronze Age Collapse*, please review at your vendor of choice.

Printed in Dunstable, United Kingdom